Albert Einstein

ALBERT EINSTEIN

Jake Goldberg

An Impact Biography

FRANKLIN WATTS
A Division of Grolier Publishing

New York London Hong Kong Sydney
Danbury, Connecticut

Photographs copyright ©: Courtesy AIP Neils Bohr Library: pp. 6 (The Hebrew University of Jerusalem), 58; The Einstein Archives: pp. 8 (both), 16, 18, 33, 35, 62, 82 top; University of New Hampshire, Lotte Jacobi Archives: pp. 9, 42; The Bettmann Archive: pp. 11, 74, 114; UPI/Bettmann: p. 79; Courtesy of Elsa Paine Mulhern: p. 14; Schweizerische Landesbibliothek: pp. 22, 25, 31, 37; AIP Emilio Segré Visual Archives: pp. 52, 71, 86, 100, 103, 111 (International Communication Agency); Ullstein Bilderdienst: p. 82 bottom (Hanns-Peter Frentz); AP/Wide World Photos: pp. 93, 98, 106; Brown Brothers: p. 94.

Library of Congress Cataloging-in-Publication Data

Goldberg, Jake, 1943–
Albert Einstein: the rebel behind relativity / by Jake Goldberg.
p.   cm. — (An impact biography)
Includes bibliographical references and index.
Summary: Describes the life and work of the scientist whose theory of relativity
revolutionized scientific thinking.
ISBN 0-531-11251-9
1. Einstein, Albert, 1875–1955—Biography—Juvenile literature. 2. Einstein, Albert, 1875–1955—Influence—Juvenile literature. 3. Relativity (Physics)—Juvenile literature. 4. Physicists—Biography—Juvenile literature. [1. Einstein, Albert, 1875–1955. 2. Physicists.] I. Title
QC16.E5G63   1996
530'.092—dc20

[B]   95-48768
                                                                         CIP
                                                                          AC

Contents

Albert Einstein at the age of four

ONE

A Slow Start

He was a chubby, shy, quiet child. One might have even called him dull. In fact, his parents worried that he might be retarded, for he could not speak fluently until he was nine years old. He would pause for a long time between sentences, as if he were rehearsing them in his mind before speaking, and sometimes he would repeat himself. He was withdrawn, though he could strike out angrily in a fit of temper, prompting his younger sister to say in later years, "a sound skull is needed to be the sister of a thinker."[1]

This seemingly backward child would grow up to be Albert Einstein, the genius who astounded the scientific world with his theory of relativity. He was born on March 14, 1879, in the small city of Ulm, in the state of Wurttemburg, in southwestern Germany. His parents, Hermann Einstein and Pauline Koch could trace their Jewish ancestors back several generations in the picturesque alpine villages of the region, which was known as Swabia.

Hermann Einstein was a jovial, easygoing man who enjoyed long alpine walks and lazy evenings in the local tavern with good friends and good German beer. He liked the

Albert's parents, Hermann and Pauline Einstein

classic German poetry of Heine and Schiller and often read it to his family in the evenings. Albert's mother had a more artistic nature than Hermann. An accomplished pianist, she loved to play for friends and relatives at evening gatherings.

When Albert was a year old, the family moved from Ulm to the much larger city of Munich in the neighboring state of Bavaria. Here Hermann Einstein entered into a business partnership with his brother, Jakob Einstein, an engineer. A few years after moving to Munich, they opened a small electrical factory that manufactured dynamos, arc lights, and electrical measuring instruments.

Munich was a city of cathedrals, art galleries, and breweries. Albert's parents hoped exposure to such varied surroundings might hasten his development. When he was only four, they sent him into the streets of the city, watching discreetly from a distance to make certain he could cross the busy intersections and find his way alone.

In 1881 Albert's sister, Maria, was born. Known to the family as Maja, she would be Albert's constant companion throughout his childhood. She later recalled that he had lit-

Albert and his sister, Maja, were close throughout their lives.

tle interest in sports, which made him dizzy, and preferred to play alone at home with building blocks.

In later years Einstein fondly remembered one incident from his early childhood. When he was five, he became entranced by a magnetic compass his father gave him. He was excited by the notion that there could be some invisible force influencing the compass needle across empty space. "I can still remember—or at least I believe I can remember—that this experience made a deep and abiding impression on me," he said.[2]

When he was six years old, Albert's mother encouraged him to study the violin. At first he found the lessons and the endless practice tedious. But in his early teens he fell in love with the music of Mozart, and it inspired him to play well. He became a competent amateur, anxious to play in family recitals when he could. The violin was to be a source of pleasure and relaxation throughout his life.

The first real intellectual stimulus came from his uncle Jakob. Since he lived next door, Jakob spent a good deal of time with Albert encouraging his interest in mathematics. "Algebra is a merry science," he told the boy. "We go hunting for a little animal whose name we don't know, so we call it x. When we bag our game, we pounce on it and give it its right name."[3] Put in the form of a game, the puzzles of mathematics appealed to Albert.

A Changing Germany

Meanwhile, great political and social changes were taking place that would eventually impact the Einsteins. A new German empire, created by Chancellor Otto von Bismarck of Prussia in 1871 in the name of Kaiser Wilhelm I, had absorbed Wurttemberg, Bavaria, and the other states of southwestern Germany. Known for their easygoing nature and their relaxed style of living, the people of southwestern Germany began to feel the intrusion of a different temperament into their lives. Gradually, the Prussian sense of military discipline, of

*After Prussia formed a new German Empire in 1871,
the Einsteins and other Germans witnessed the strict discipline
of the new government in parades of
marching soldiers.*

obedience, efficiency, and punctuality, took hold. Politicians
and civil servants began wearing military-style uniforms.

The troops of the new empire were frequently on parade.
Unlike many other boys, young Albert avoided the parades,
instinctively fearing the rows of men marching like mindless
robots. But for many Germans the sense of belonging to a
powerful new nation was intoxicating.

The new Germany underwent a period of rapid industrialization. With the help of some of the finest scientific minds and technical institutes in Europe, German factories were quick to put the latest discoveries to good use. Most of these discoveries came out of the new sciences of chemistry and electricity. The Germans were becoming leaders in the manufacture of nitrates for fertilizers and explosives, in the production of new chemicals for bleaches, dyes, inks, pharmaceutical products, and plastics, and in the construction of electric generators, batteries, switches, insulated wires, telegraph cables, and scientific instruments.

The domination of German industry by large firms such as Siemens, I. G. Farben, and Krupp made it difficult for Hermann Einstein's modest electric business to survive. Siemens's development of the modern electric generator in 1867 revolutionized electric technology. The generator, known as a *dynamo*, can produce a continuous supply of electricity as it rotates. As a result of this invention, industrial machinery and railways became electrified, and electric lights began to appear on streets and in private homes.

The Einsteins admired the achievements of the new Germany, but with reservations. They had little use for the autocratic mindset of the Prussians, and they could not help worrying about new stirrings of anti-Jewish feeling in the nation. The Jews were blamed for a serious financial crisis in 1873, and, in the year of Einstein's birth, a man named Wilhelm Marr founded the League of Anti-Semites.

The Einsteins were frequently reminded that many Germans harbored a strong prejudice against them, even though they regarded themselves as secular German citizens. Like many German Jews of the time, the Einsteins had abandoned most Jewish religious beliefs and observances, and maintained a cultural, rather than a religious, Jewish identity.

Out of convenience, Albert attended a nearby Catholic elementary school. All the elementary schools in Germany at the time were organized by religious denomination, and Catholic schools predominated in the city because most of

Munich's residents were Catholic. The Einsteins were free thinkers and cared little about the teaching of religion as long as the school was a good one.

Albert was exposed to the doctrines of Catholicism at school, and at home he learned the tenets of Judaism from a relative, though his father regarded these beliefs as "ancient superstitions." For a brief time, Albert became deeply religious and practiced the orthodox Jewish customs that his parents had forsaken.

A Distaste for School

In 1889, at age ten, Albert entered the Luitpold Gymnasium. In Europe, a *gymnasium* is a high school that prepares students for college. He excelled at physics and mathematics and earned good grades in most of his subjects, but he made few friends and hated sports. He also disliked the emphasis on classical culture and the rote learning of Greek and Latin grammar.

He developed a strong distaste for the Prussian-influenced mode of education. Teachers were stern and dictatorial and kept their distance from their students, who were expected to demonstrate humility, obedience, and discipline. Much of the teaching was through endless mechanical drill; questioning and discussion were discouraged.

Years later Einstein wrote, "The teachers in the elementary school appeared to me like sergeants, and the gymnasium teachers like lieutenants."[4] His experience at the gymnasium only strengthened his hatred of the martial spirit of German society. "The over-emphasized military mentality in the German State was alien to me even as a boy," he wrote.[5] Einstein felt a need to experiment intellectually without restraint, and he recognized that real learning, for him at any rate, would have to take place outside school through self-study.

That process of self-study was accelerated by one of the few Jewish customs Albert's parents maintained—the practice

Max Talmud introduced twelve-year-old Albert to popular science books.

of inviting a young Jewish student to dinner once a week. When Albert was twelve, a medical student at Munich University named Max Talmud began to show up for dinner on Thursday nights. Talmud, who later changed his name to Talmey, noted Albert's keen interest in physics and mathematics and began supplying him with popular scientific textbooks. These books were a revelation to Albert, and he quickly abandoned his flirtation with orthodox Judaism and religious explanations for natural phenomena.

His reading and self-study had a great impact on Albert. "The consequence was a positively fanatic orgy of free-thinking coupled with the impression that youth is intentionally being deceived by the state through lies; it was a crushing impression," he wrote in later years.[6] Thus, Einstein became even more convinced that the state-sponsored educational system discouraged independent thinking.

Einstein was particularly impressed by a geometry book he was given. He later called it his "holy geometry book." The process of making logical proofs concerning lines, shapes, and angles fascinated Einstein. It made him skeptical toward all assertions not proven with logic, including much of what he had been taught by the schools, the state, and the Bible.

Though he abandoned his faith in the dogmas of religion, it could be said that he retained the religious impulse—the desire to know the answers to the great questions of existence. It wasn't long before the young man had surpassed both Talmud and the gymnasium's curriculum in his understanding of modern scientific problems.

In 1894, when Albert was fifteen, his father's business began to fail. The Einsteins decided to reestablish the factory in Pavia, near Milan in Italy. They had wealthy relatives in nearby Genoa who could be counted on for support if necessary. Albert's parents and his uncle Jakob moved to Italy, leaving Albert alone in a boarding house to finish his schooling in Munich.

Without a supportive home environment, Albert felt even more keenly the regimentation of the gymnasium and was determined to resist it. His classmates sensed his detachment and his teachers sensed defiance in the questions he refused to stop asking. His Greek teacher told him, "Your mere presence spoils the respect of the class for me."[7] Within two months of his parents' departure, Albert and the school's authorities apparently decided that it would be best if he left the gymnasium.

It was a bold decision to leave school without a diploma, as this would make it almost impossible for Einstein to enter a German university. In anticipation of that problem, he secured a note from a local doctor stating that he had suf-

Albert and Maja before the Einsteins moved to Italy.

fered an illness that required him to leave school. Then he obtained another note from his mathematics teacher stating that his knowledge of the subject qualified him for advanced study even without a gymnasium degree.

His parents were upset by Albert's decision, but he assured them that he would study hard so that he could pass the test for admission to college. The depth of his hatred for the authoritarian atmosphere he had endured became apparent when he arrived in Italy and told his father he wanted to legally renounce his German citizenship. By doing so, he could also avoid being drafted into the Prussian army—a real danger if he were to return to Germany. After some prodding, his father agreed to file the papers for him.

TWO

GLIMMERS OF LIGHT

For a time in Italy, the problem of further schooling did not trouble Einstein. He was intoxicated by the relaxed pace of life and the natural spontaneity of the Italian people, so different from what he had experienced in Germany. Einstein immersed himself in the country's art galleries, its Renaissance architecture, and in the emotional and melodic music that filled every opera house and market square. He enjoyed long walks through the Italian countryside to his relatives' home in Genoa, on the Mediterranean coast.

But he did not forget his scientific studies. During this period, Albert sent his first scientific paper to his uncle in Genoa. Written in 1895 when he was about sixteen years old, it was a sophisticated essay on magnetism, the subject that had first attracted him to science. He was clearly familiar with the theory of electromagnetism, which had only recently been put forth by the Scottish physicist James Clerk Maxwell, in the late 1860s.

Before Maxwell's theory, physicists had assumed that electricity and magnetism are two distinct forces that operate independently of each other. But Maxwell concluded that

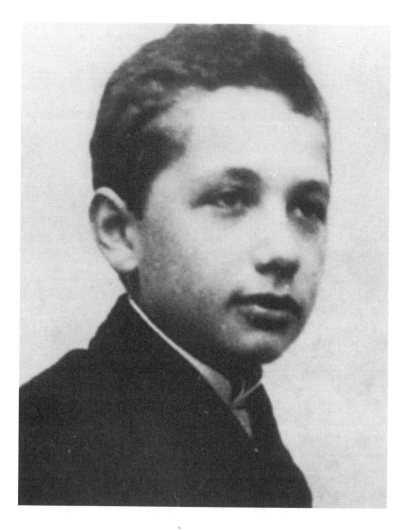

Albert around the age of fourteen

they are actually part of a single phenomenon called *electro-magnetism*. Electricity and magnetism are two sides of the same coin. Wherever one exists, the other must be present, and a change in one produces a change in the other.

The theory seemed to explain the workings of the dynamos that had recently been developed. In light of the theory, it made sense that dynamos could generate electricity in a coil of wire rotating in a *magnetic field*, the extent in space of a magnet's attractive force. In reality, a magnet, as well as a wire carrying electricity, generates an *electromagnetic field* that extends into the surrounding space.

Maxwell's equations indicated that such fields could travel like a wave through space at a speed virtually identical to the speed of light. Thus, Maxwell concluded, light must actually consist of electromagnetic waves radiating through space. This was the most startling revelation of Maxwell's theory. Light and the energy from a magnet or from a wire conducting electricity are different forms of the same thing. The only difference is in the length of the waves.

Einstein's essay mentioned the experiments of the physicist Heinrich Hertz in 1888, which proved Maxwell was right. Hertz discovered radio waves, another form of electromagnetic radiation, and found that they conform to Maxwell's theory. Radio waves have a wavelength longer than that of visible light. Eventually, other forms of electromagnetic radiation with shorter wavelengths than visible light would be discovered, including ultraviolet radiation, X rays, and gamma rays.

The subject of Einstein's 1895 essay, which was never published, was the substance on which electromagnetic waves were thought to travel. Although it had never been detected, physicists at the time assumed that it must exist, because all their experience with other kinds of waves told them that waves cannot travel through empty space. Ocean waves travel through water, sound waves travel through air, and the seismic waves of earthquakes travel through the ground. In fact, waves are actually just a disturbance or vibration in a substance, or *medium*. What, then, vibrates as light travels through the emptiness of outer space? Maxwell proposed that light travels on something called *ether*, an idea that scientists had toyed with since the time of Aristotle.

Maxwell's luminiferous, or "light-carrying," ether was not a material substance in the usual sense. People could walk through it with no effect. Earth moved through the ether,

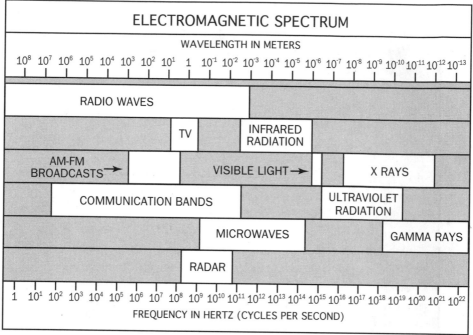

Source: Encyclopedia Americana

Figure 1. The electromagnetic spectrum includes visible light, radio waves, X rays, and energy of many other different wavelengths. The frequency of the energy is the number of waves that pass per second.

but experienced no "drag" from it. Yet somehow the ether filled all space and carried the vibrations of electromagnetic energy.

Einstein speculated on the behavior of the ether in a magnetic field generated by a wire conducting electricity. In so doing, he guessed correctly that conductors resist changes in current, a property called *self-inductance*. He did not call it that, however, for he was unaware that physicists had just recently discovered and named it. This was the first inkling of the brilliance that was to come from the teenager.

Back to School

Einstein's idyllic period in Italy lasted only a year. His father expected him to finish his education, with a degree in engineering perhaps, and then join the family business. Albert, however, hoped for a career in theoretical physics. Whatever his course of study, he had to get back into school.

He was interested in attending an excellent advanced technical college in Switzerland, later known as the Eidgenossiche Technische Hochschule (ETH)—in English, the Federal Polytechnic Institute. It was located in the predominantly German-speaking city of Zurich.

In the fall of 1895 Einstein traveled to Zurich to take the ETH entrance examination, but he failed the sections of the test dealing with foreign languages, zoology, and botany. He did so well in physics and mathematics, however, that he impressed the head of the ETH, Heinrich Weber. Weber suggested that he get his gymnasium degree at the Swiss Cantonal School in nearby Aarau, after which he would be eligible for admission to the ETH.

Einstein was apprehensive about going back to school and repeating the oppressive experience of his years in Munich. But the Swiss Cantonal School proved to be very different from the Luitpold Gymnasium. Here there was much less emphasis on discipline and the teachers and students were allowed to fraternize with each other in an atmosphere of free discussion. There was a fine new physics laboratory, and students were encouraged to conduct their own experiments.

Einstein stayed in the home of one of the headmasters, Professor Jost Winteler, whose son Paul would later marry Einstein's sister, Maja. Einstein's physics teacher, August Tuschmid, was excellent, and he gave the young man a thorough grounding in the theories of modern physics. The electromagnetic theory, in particular, percolated through Einstein's mind at the Cantonal School and for years afterward.

Einstein met Mileva Maric, his first wife, at the university in Zurich.

After his graduation in 1896, Einstein returned to Zurich from Aarau. The ETH waved its age requirement and Einstein was admitted at the age of sixteen. He formally enrolled in a program designed to prepare students to become teachers of physics and mathematics.

Zurich proved to be a cosmopolitan city with a lively intellectual climate. Einstein lived the typical life of a poor university student, moving from one rooming house to another, eating at inexpensive cafes, and joining other students for walks and outings in the Swiss Alps. He was supported by his Genoese relatives, who sent him 100 francs a month. From this sum he set aside 20 francs a month to save for the fee required to apply for Swiss citizenship. He made formal application for citizenship in 1899, and the Swiss granted it in 1901.

Socially, Einstein blossomed in Zurich. He lost some of his shyness and grew into a handsome, self-assured young man who was popular with young women. His attraction to the abstract problems of physics, however, set him apart from all but a few of his close friends. At the ETH, Einstein met Mileva Maric, a physics student of Serbian ancestry, who would become his first wife in 1903.

Einstein had several excellent teachers at the school, notably Hermann Minkowski, a mathematician who would later make an important contribution to relativity theory. But on the whole he found the classes and lectures boring, and his hatred of the academic environment returned.

Most of the instructors were scientifically conservative. They taught the laws of force and motion developed by the seventeenth-century physicists Galileo and Isaac Newton and avoided the growing body of experimental knowledge that raised questions about whether these laws applied in the areas of electricity, magnetism, and light. Einstein was frustrated to find that Maxwell's theory of electromagnetism was not even discussed by some of the professors.

Einstein stopped attending lectures. To pass his exams, he studied the elaborate notes taken by his friend Marcel Grossman. In contrast to Einstein, Grossman was a model student, liked by all his professors. Despite their personality differences, a lifetime friendship developed between the two based on their love of discussing physics with each other.

Instead of attending lectures, Einstein busied himself conducting experiments in the laboratory and reading, on his own, the writings of the physicists Hertz, Hermann Helmholtz, and Gustav Kirchoff. In his second year at the school, Einstein became absorbed with the problem of detecting the ether. He realized that if the ether existed, the motion of objects should be able to be measured with respect to it. He wanted to construct a device that would measure the movement of Earth through the ether, but his teachers discouraged him, and he never found the time to carry it out.

Here again, Einstein was on the cutting edge of science, for leading physicists at the time were trying to detect the ether. Remarkably, he was unaware of their efforts when he conceived his idea. One experiment conducted in 1887 by Albert Michelson and Edward Morley is famous today for providing evidence that the ether did not exist. Their device, known as the Michelson-Morley interferometer, was ingeniously designed to detect the movement of Earth through the ether (see box on pages 26–27.) But they found no evidence of the ether.

Many scientists at the time maintained that the ether existed, but that for some reason motion through it was undetectable. With no evidence of the ether, Maxwell's theory of electromagnetism remained incomplete. A great mystery blocked further progress toward a complete understanding of the nature of light.

A Chink in Newton's Armor

In addition to Marcel Grossman, Einstein met another lifelong friend in Zurich, Michele Angelo Besso, an engineering student from Italy. Besso introduced Einstein to the book *Science of Mechanics*, by the Austrian physicist Ernst Mach. It concerned how bodies move in response to forces, a field of science called *mechanics*. The book left a great impression on Einstein and started his mind churning about relativity. Mach boldly criticized Newton's view of the relative motion of objects, and for this, Einstein later praised Mach's "incorruptible scepticism and independence."[1]

Because the ideas of Galileo and Newton had been such a great leap forward for science, many nineteenth-century physicists accepted all their theories unquestioningly. But Mach believed that many of their theories were based on untestable ideas. In formulating his laws of motion, for example, Newton invented the concepts of *absolute space* and

*A friend of Einstein's, Michele Angelo Besso,
introduced him to the groundbreaking ideas of
physicist Ernst Mach.*

absolute time as reference points from which to measure motion. But neither he nor anyone else, Mach pointed out, had any idea of how to locate them.

Newton's purpose in creating these concepts was to account for Galileo's principle of relativity. Galileo said that all motion is relative; even though a man may appear to be walking from our perspective, his motion is very different from the perspective of the Sun. So Newton stipulated that his laws were valid in the frame of reference of absolute space, which he defined as the immovable volume of space created by God. He defined a similarly cosmic absolute time, begin-

In 1887, Albert Michelson and Edward Morley, at what is now Case Western Reserve University in Cleveland, constructed a very sensitive device to find evidence of the ether. Michelson reasoned that Earth must move through the ether at about 18 miles per second as it travels in its orbit around the Sun. Consequently, an "ether wind" must be flowing through Earth in a direction opposite Earth's motion. If light waves travel in the ether, then light moving with the ether wind should travel faster than light moving across, or perpendicular to, the ether wind.

The device, built by Morley, compared the speeds of light moving in these two directions by splitting a beam in half and sending each half along the same distance in different directions. As shown in the diagram on the next page, part of the beam went to mirror C and the other part to mirror D. The halves were then rejoined and sent to a viewing telescope. Any difference in speed between the two halves as they traveled separate paths could be determined by examining the pattern of interference between the waves of light when they recombined.

When rejoined, the light waves added together, producing a pattern of dark and light lines determined by how far the waves have shifted in time. This phenomenon of interference was one of the first clues scientists had that light is a wave. Theoretically, there would be no interference pattern if the difference in speed is zero, because the waveforms would coincide precisely. But imperfections in the mirrors and other components along the two pathways introduced a slight offset between the waves. Realizing this, the experimenters rotated their device 90 degrees and looked for any *change* in the interference pattern from one position to the other.

No matter how Michelson oriented the device, which he called an *interferometer,* the interference pattern did not change. The speed of light appeared to be constant in both directions; in other words, he could not detect the ether.

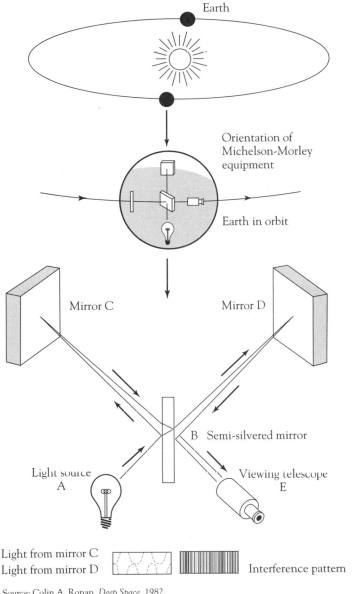

Earth

Orientation of
Michelson-Morley
equipment

Earth in orbit

Mirror C   Mirror D

B Semi-silvered mirror

Light source   Viewing telescope
A   E

Light from mirror C
Light from mirror D   Interference pattern

Source: Colin A. Ronan, *Deep Space*, 1982.

*Figure 2. The interferometer designed by Michelson and
Morley measured the distance light traveled in two
perpendicular directions.*

ning with the birth of the universe and continuing steadily forever.

But, Mach pointed out, scientists would never be able to pinpoint these frames of reference. He argued that scientific theories should be based only on observable phenomena—that is, phenomena that scientists can measure and accurately describe. So even though Newton's laws work in our experience, Mach insisted that there is no proof that they are *universal* laws, as Newton claimed. Furthermore, Mach believed that any attempt to formulate a universal law is wasted effort. Einstein's own yearning for deep, meaningful, universal laws of nature led him to disagree with Mach on this point. Nonetheless, to the end of his life, Einstein praised Mach as a major influence on his work.

The skepticism and independence that Einstein admired so much in Mach were qualities that Einstein himself possessed in great measure. He could be very reserved and withdrawn at times, but he could also be stubborn, defiant, and determined. He had a way of making his displeasure known to teachers without quite going beyond the bounds of propriety. Einstein grew increasingly frustrated by the inadequate explanations given to him by his professors, and he did not make many friends among the faculty. Even Professor Heinrich Weber, who had encouraged Einstein to enroll at the ETH, turned against him, saying, "You're a clever fellow! But you have one fault. You won't let anyone tell you a thing."[2]

When Einstein graduated in August 1900, he was somewhat shocked to find that the ETH did not offer him a position. It was customary for the school to offer the brighter students employment as research assistants after graduation, and the three other students who passed the final exam all received offers. But Einstein had offended too many people, especially Weber, whom he had refused to address by the proper title "Herr Professor." After Einstein graduated, his Genoese relatives stopped sending money, so at the age of twenty-one, he desperately needed to find a means of supporting himself.

For a while, Einstein was genuinely adrift, earning a little money by tutoring students in mathematics and physics. Years later he wrote that the antagonism he felt toward the teaching methods at the ETH and the pressure of preparing for examinations had made "the consideration of any scientific problems distasteful to me for an entire year."[3]

Still, he managed to publish a scientific paper in December 1900 in the prestigious German scientific journal *Annalen der Physik*. Titled "Deductions from the Phenomena of Capillarity," it was a minor paper on capillary action, the tendency of liquids to rise along the walls of very narrow tubes. He sent copies of the paper to the German chemist Wilhelm Ostwald at the University of Leipzig in Germany and to the Dutch physicist Kamerlingh Onnes at the University of Leiden in Holland. He hoped they would offer him a research assistantship, but no offer was made. Einstein suspected that Heinrich Weber had conspired against him by spreading the word not to hire his rebellious and disobedient former pupil. Whatever the reasons, his hopes for a secure position in a university were fading rapidly.

On February 21, 1901, Einstein officially became a Swiss citizen, but he was still without employment prospects. It wasn't until mid-May that he secured a temporary position at a technical school in Winterthur, about ten miles northeast of Zurich. He substituted for a mathematics instructor who had to go into military service. Here, Einstein wrote another scientific paper on the thermodynamic properties of gases.

In July 1901, with the return of the regular mathematics teacher, Einstein was again out of work. Through another friend and fellow ETH student, Conrad Habicht, Einstein secured employment at a boarding school in the town of Schaffhausen on the northern Swiss border with Germany. His job was to tutor a young student from England, but he soon came into conflict with his employer, who demanded the rigorous teaching methods Einstein had come to hate. By the end of 1901, Einstein was dismissed.

Einstein was next rescued by Marcel Grossman, the young man who had taken lecture notes for him at the ETH. Grossman, an assistant professor at the ETH at the time, spoke to his father about Einstein, and Grossman's father spoke to Friedrich Haller, the director of the Swiss patent office in Bern. In December 1901 Einstein traveled to Bern and met with Haller for two hours. It was obvious that Einstein lacked the technical qualifications for the patent office, but the young man's intelligence impressed him. In any case, Haller wanted to do a favor for the Grossmans.

Einstein formally applied for the position of technical expert, third class, and in February 1902 he moved to Bern to await the outcome of Haller's decision, supporting himself with more tutoring jobs. Finally, in June 1902, Haller invited him to begin work at the patent office at a modest salary of 3,500 Swiss francs. It was Einstein's first steady job, and a secure civil service job at that. He could settle down, support himself, and devote his spare time to his own studies. Toward the end of his life, Einstein expressed his gratitude for Grossman's help, saying it was the greatest thing he had ever done for him.

Throughout his college years and during the search for work afterward, the problems associated with Maxwell's theory of electromagnetism never left Einstein's mind. It is not clear whether he was directly aware of the results of the Michelson-Morley experiment at this time. His later recollections on this point are vague and contradictory. But at some point during this time, he became aware of the work of a Dutch physicist named Hendrik Lorentz, who refined Maxwell's theory in the 1890s by interpreting his equations in terms of charged particles traveling in an electrical current.

As he settled into his new life as clerk in the patent office in Bern, Einstein began to devote more and more attention to the problem. He knew that something was fundamentally wrong with the Newtonian world view, and all his experiences as a student led him to distrust established authority. The general laws of motion were the commandments pushed

Marcel Grossman helped Einstein get his first steady job, at the Swiss patent office.

upon him by teachers he had no faith in. If the whole theoretical structure of modern science had to come down, Einstein had no reservations about swinging the wrecking ball. But he would struggle with the problem for several more years before developing the theory that would make him famous.

THREE

A BURST OF CREATIVITY

The city of Bern, situated on the Aare River, was the official political center of Switzerland. The Swiss Parliament, many government bureaus, including the patent office, and the embassies of many European countries were located here. Gothic churches, beautiful fountains and bridges, and narrow lanes gave the city a medieval flavor popular with tourists. In 1902, when Einstein arrived, it was just beginning to flourish as a ski resort as well. The surrounding region contained some of Switzerland's finest mountains and lakes.

Einstein took a small, poorly furnished apartment not far from the city's famous Clock Tower. His duties at the patent office involved evaluating patent applications submitted by inventors who wanted their designs legally protected from unauthorized copying. Many of these inventors were amateur tinkerers, and the descriptions of their inventions were often poorly written and sometimes simply ridiculous. Schemes for perpetual motion machines that ran forever without using energy were common.

Einstein's job was to analyze the invention, identify the essential principles behind it, determine whether it would

*Einstein in the patent office
around 1905*

work, and rewrite the application in clear and precise technical language if it deserved further consideration. The work was not without interest or value for him, for it continually challenged his analytical and conceptual powers.

He did his daily work conscientiously, but occasionally he couldn't resist working on his own scientific problem. He would hide his notes in his desk when someone passed his office. Even decades later, he felt guilty whenever he thought about this deception. After work, in the evenings and on weekends, Einstein turned his full attention to the paradoxes of modern physics. The patent job was a comfortable arrangement for a young man whose quiet defiance and stubbornness had cost him a conventional academic career.

It was not long, however, before Einstein received a serious personal shock. In the fall of 1902 his father was stricken with heart disease, and Einstein returned to Milan in October to be present for his death. His parents had always been warm and nurturing, even throughout his problems with the state and schools. Albert had felt terrible about being a financial burden to his family during his school years and the jobless period afterward. When his father died at the age of fifty-five, Albert felt a deep sense of guilt, perhaps suspecting that the financial stress his father had been under was in some way responsible.

In 1903 he started his own family by marrying Mileva Maric, his fellow student from the ETH. Recently, documents have revealed that Mileva and Albert had a daughter in January 1902 before they were married. Although it seems that they originally planned to keep the child, whom they named Lieserl, they gave her up for some unknown reason. She may have been adopted by distant relatives, but her fate has not been discovered.

Their second child, Hans Albert, was born in 1904, and another son, Eduard, was born in 1910. The couple were happy together at first, but the marriage developed problems. Perhaps they stemmed from the stress and shame of concealing an illegitimate child, or from the fact that Albert's

Mileva, with Eduard on the left and Hans Albert on the right, in 1914, the year the Einsteins separated

mother never approved of Mileva as a wife for her son. His mother felt that Mileva's Serbian background was beneath him, a prejudice shared by many Germans at the time.

A nother possible reason is that Mileva began to lose interest in science as Albert's interest became more and more obsessive. To Einstein, Mileva seemed stern and reserved, unexcited by his passion for physics. To Mileva, Einstein must have seemed self-absorbed. Though he dutifully cared for and played with his children, his mind was often elsewhere. A year before they separated in 1914, Mileva wrote to a friend that Albert now lived only for his science and paid little attention to the family. In divorce papers, she accused him of having an extramarital affair with the woman who would become his second wife. Years later, Einstein would frankly admit that he had not been the best of husbands.

The Olympia Academy

The scientific discussions with his close friends was what Einstein most enjoyed about the early years in Bern. During these sessions, Einstein shed his shyness and revealed something of his father's jovial nature. He became relaxed, forthright, humorous, and dominant in these discussions. Conrad Habicht was in Bern, and so was Maurice Solovine, a Rumanian student of philosophy whom Einstein tutored. Forming what they called the "Olympia Academy," the three men met regularly to discuss physics, philosophy, art, music, or whatever else interested them. They usually met in Einstein's apartment and continued their discussions late into the night.

In 1904 Michele Besso came to Bern and joined the group after taking a job at the patent office, at Einstein's suggestion. Continuing their Academy discussions during pleasant walks to and from work, Einstein and Besso became especially close. But the Academy lasted only about two years, because by 1905 Habicht and Solovine had left Bern. Besso remained, serving as a sounding board for Einstein's evolving ideas.

Between 1902 and 1904, Einstein published a number of scientific papers in the *Annalen der Physik*. They were minor but important contributions to the newly emerging kinetic theory of matter, which held that many of the characteristics of matter could be explained by the arrangement and energetic motions, or *kinetics*, of atoms and molecules. The theory said, for instance, that the heat inside matter comes from the rapid oscillations and collisions of these particles. In 1902 there was no direct evidence that atoms and molecules existed, even though working chemists operated as if they did.

Einstein was aware that before he died in 1879, James Clerk Maxwell and the Austrian physicist Ludwig Boltzmann had been working on a formula for the temperature and pressure of a gas based on the average speed of its molecules. They applied Newton's laws of motion to billions of tiny particles to prove that their motion causes heat and pressure. Because the calculations involved finding the average motion of many molecules, this field of study was later known as *statistical*

The founding members of the "Olympia Academy" were Conrad Habicht, Maurice Solovine, and Einstein.

mechanics. Einstein's papers offered mathematical and conceptual support for the kinetic theory of matter and the existence of atoms, though later he judged most of his work before 1905 to be of negligible value.

In 1905, everything changed. Einstein wrote six scientific papers that year, three of revolutionary import. It was an extraordinary burst of creativity, and his work covered a variety of subjects. One of Einstein's biographers, Abraham Pais, a physicist who was his colleague and friend in later years, has speculated that the birth of Hans Albert in 1904 may have inspired Einstein's creativity.

His first paper of 1905, "On a Heuristic Point of View Regarding the Production and Transformation of Light," was completed on March 17. In a letter to Habicht, Einstein described it as "very revolutionary," but it was not about relativity. The paper was a contribution to another scientific revolution involving the motions of particles in the realm of the very small. This revolution would eventually, for subatomic particles, replace classical Newtonian mechanics with something called *quantum mechanics*.

His paper explained the peculiar results of an experiment conducted by the German physicist Philipp Lenard in 1902. Lenard was investigating the photoelectric effect, a phenomenon that occurs when light shines on a piece of thin metal. The light knocks electrons from the surface of the metal. Lenard tried increasing the intensity—the brightness—of the light striking the metal to see whether the electrons were ejected with greater velocities, as he expected. But their velocities did not change. Faster electrons were ejected only when he shortened the wavelength of the light. As the wavelength shortens, the number of waves that pass per second—the frequency of the light—increases.

Einstein explained Lenard's unexpected result in terms of *quanta*, an idea put forward in 1900 by Max Planck, a physicist working at the University of Berlin. Planck's idea was so radical that physicists did not accept it at first. Even Planck himself had a hard time believing it, but it worked so well in explaining blackbody radiation (see box on p. 40) that he published it anyway. His idea was that energy is emitted and absorbed by objects in tiny chunks called quanta. It is as if the transfer of energy, on a very small scale, is digitized like the information in a computer. Until then, energy had always been thought of flowing to and from matter continuously.

Einstein's first 1905 paper granted legitimacy to Planck's interpretation. Einstein said that light is actually made up of quanta whose energy content, or "size," depends on the frequency of the light. When the light on the metal was made more intense, the metal was bombarded by more quanta of the same size, none of which had the "push" to knock out electrons any faster. But when the frequency of the light was increased, "bigger" quanta were created that could knock out electrons at higher speeds.

In putting forward his quantum hypothesis, Einstein was clearly going beyond Planck. Einstein was suggesting not only that energy is emitted and absorbed in tiny bundles, but that the light waves themselves are made up of energy bundles. He eventually came to see these light-quanta as particles, and they became known as *photons*. They were, in effect, wave-particles, a new and strange physical entity.

In 1918 Planck was awarded the Nobel Prize for his theory of the quantum. When Einstein won his Nobel Prize in 1921, it was not for relativity, but for the paper on the photoelectric effect. Quantum theory would eventually evolve into a comprehensive explanation of the behavior of matter on the subatomic level. Ironically, Einstein would later object to many of its conclusions.

The second of the papers Einstein wrote that year was the least important. "A New Determination of Molecular Dimensions," completed on April 30, examined the way sugar molecules diffuse through water and offered a method of inferring the size of the molecules from their behavior. This was a further contribution to the kinetic theory of matter. He sent the paper to Professor Alfred Kleiner of the University of Zurich as his doctoral dissertation, but Kleiner rejected it as too short. Einstein revised it, adding only one sentence, and Kleiner accepted the "longer" version. Thus, in 1905 Einstein was awarded his doctorate, and the revised paper was published in the *Annalen der Physik* in 1906.

He continued his defense of the kinetic theory of matter in his third paper of 1905, received at the offices of the *Annalen der Physik* on May 11. In it, Einstein tackled the problem of *Brownian motion*, named after the Scottish botanist Robert Brown who discovered the phenomenon in 1828. Brown found that specks of dust or pollen grains placed in an undisturbed liquid exhibit tiny, jerky, random motions—Brownian motion. According to the kinetic theory, the movement of the specks was caused by the average forces of millions of atoms jostling against them, but there was no proof of this.

The seeds of the quantum mechanics revolution were experiments conducted in the late nineteenth century on blackbody radiation. A blackbody is a theoretical, idealized body that completely absorbs all the light that falls on it, with no reflection. In reality, black objects may come close to totally absorbing all wavelengths, but there is always some reflection. When a true blackbody is heated to incandescence—until it glows—and held at a steady temperature, it radiates light at all wavelengths, since it absorbs all wavelengths. Physicists hoped that studying blackbodies would give them a better understanding of how ordinary objects radiate light energy.

They found that they could approximate the light radiating from a blackbody by the light emerging from a tiny hole in a metal furnace. The temperature of this furnace determined the colors of light that would emanate from it, just as objects change color when they become very hot. As objects heat up, they turn from red to orange to yellow, and if they become extremely hot, they even turn white, blue-white, or violet.

This happens because our eyes detect the changing wavelengths of the light waves as a change in color. Every color of the rainbow has a wavelength of electromagnetic radiation corresponding to it. Red light has the longest wavelength, and violet has the shortest. Shorter wavelengths of electromagnetic radiation, such as ultraviolet radiation, are invisible to the eye. As more energy is added to the light waves, they vibrate faster; their wavelength decreases and their frequency increases.

Einstein worked out formulas for calculating the probable movement of the specks over time, assuming that the kinetic theory was correct. The formulas worked, and this paper, the culmination of Einstein's work with kinetic theory and statistical mechanics, was a powerful argument in

Hot objects at a steady temperature emit many wavelengths of visible and nonvisible light, of varying amounts. The color we see is the wavelength that predominates over other colors. The experimenters measured the amount of light at each wavelength coming from the blackbody, or furnace, held at different temperatures. They knew that if light is really made up of continuously flowing waves of different frequencies, as Maxwell suggested, then a blackbody should emit light equally at all frequencies. In other words, for a given temperature, the intensity of each color should be the same. But the experiments showed that hot objects emit very little high-frequency, violet and ultraviolet light compared with lower frequency light. At a loss to explain this, physicists called the problem the "violet catastrophe."

In studying the problem, Max Planck found that he could accurately predict the distribution of frequencies by assuming a radical idea: the electromagnetic radiation, though wavelike in form, was being *emitted* from the body in little spurts or chunks. These chunks of energy were proportional to the frequency of the radiation. The amount of energy in a chunk could be calculated by multiplying the frequency by a constant, *h,* known as Planck's constant. Low-frequency light emits energy in small chunks and high-frequency light emits energy in large chunks. Since it takes more energy to produce large chunks, the small chunks—lower-frequency light—predominate. Planck called these particlelike bundles of energy *quanta*.

favor of the existence of atoms and the idea that their movements are the source of heat.

If Einstein had stopped with these three papers, he would have been considered a great physicist. But his fourth paper would make him the greatest physicist of the twentieth century.

Einstein's mind was a laboratory in which he conducted thought experiments.

FOUR

THE SPECIAL THEORY

In June 1905 Einstein completed his fourth paper of the year. It was published, along with his papers on the photoelectric effect and Brownian motion, in volume 17, series four, of *Annalen der Physik*. (This volume has become a highly prized collector's item.) The new paper, entitled "On the Electrodynamics of Moving Bodies," was Einstein's daring announcement of the theory of special relativity, his answer to problems that had puzzled him for almost ten years.

Driven to radical conclusions about the nature of space and time, he was left in a state of nervous exhaustion when he finished it. It had taken an intense mental struggle and enormous courage for a twenty-six-year-old civil servant unrecognized in the scientific community to challenge 200 years of experience with physical laws. Einstein reduced Newton's laws of motion to a useful approximation of reality, accurate only for motion people come across in everyday situations.

The theory of space and time Einstein introduced came to be known as the special theory of relativity, because it dealt only with the special case of motion in frames of reference that are neither accelerating nor decelerating with respect to the observer. In other words, the frames of reference are either stationary or moving at a constant speed in a straight line. These are called *inertial frames of reference*. Einstein's goal was to explain the strange behavior of light when an inertial frame of reference is moving at or near the speed of light.

He had actually begun thinking about this problem when he was a sixteen-year-old student in Aarau. At that time, he had tried to imagine what would happen if he could run after a light wave at the same speed as the wave. Einstein concluded that according to Newton's theory, he would see a stationary wave of light, but he doubted that such a thing was possible.

This was the start of the unique approach Einstein took to the problem of electromagnetism. Rather than conducting experiments and then analyzing the results as most physicists did, he put the problem into the form of what he called a "thought experiment," an experiment conducted in the mind. A thought experiment was necessary because the scope or scale of the problem was so large that actual experimentation was impractical.

By 1905 the thought experiment had matured, and Einstein had reached a startling conclusion. His teenage attempt had been inconclusive because he had clung to the Newtonian view of relativity, which assumed that velocities are additive. If a man on a train moving at 50 miles per hour throws a ball toward the front of the train at 30 miles an hour, an observer by the side of the track would measure the speed of the ball as 80 miles per hour. And if the observer could run along the track at 80 miles an hour, he would see the ball as stationary.

But this logic did not seem to hold at the speed of light— if light was indeed a wave, as Maxwell had found. A stationary wave would not appear to be a wave at all. A wave had to propagate, to move outward from its point of origin, and to oscillate, or it would cease to exist. Einstein was convinced that an observer traveling at the speed of light would still see light.

But if this observer could see light traveling ahead of him, would not a stationary observer measure those light waves as moving faster than the speed of light? Einstein concluded that this was impossible, according to Maxwell's equations. No matter how fast an object moves toward or away from the observer, light from that object would always appear to travel at a constant speed—186,000 miles per second. This idea was a clear violation of the Newtonian view.

Einstein began his paper by dispensing with the idea of the ether. He said that the ether is not necessary to carry light waves. There is no invisible substance spread throughout the universe, representing an absolute frame of reference. Einstein said that any frame of reference is an equally valid point from which to measure motion elsewhere. There is no favored position, no universal frame of reference, no cosmic yardstick, no absolute space in any sense. All motion within the universe is relative, a comparison of motion between two frames of references.

But no matter what the frame of reference, the speed of light in a vacuum is always the same; it is a fundamental constant of nature. Light emanating from an object moving rapidly toward an observer moves at 186,000 miles per second, no faster, and light from an object moving rapidly away from an observer also moves at 186,000 miles per second, no slower. Light does not partake of the motion of material objects. When in a vacuum, it cannot be pushed by any force to go faster or retarded by any force to go slower—unlike all the material objects of the universe.

The ramifications of accepting an unvarying speed of light were immense. It meant that as an object approaches the speed of light, it appears to shrink in size and increase in *mass*, or matter. At the speed of light, the mass and force required to accelerate the body become infinite. If the length of the body is reduced to zero and its mass is increased to infinity, it follows that no material object could ever attain the speed of light and still exist.

And Einstein went even further than that. He reasoned

that time itself varies between reference frames whose relative speed approaches the speed of light. The faster a system moves with respect to an observer in another system, the more the measurement of time in each of the two systems would disagree. To both observers, time would appear to be slower in the other reference frame, and when the relative speed reached the speed of light, time would seem to stand still (see box on p. 48). The effect, Einstein said, occurs to some extent at all speeds, but because everything in our experience moves so slowly with respect to the speed of light, the disagreements between clocks are too small to notice.

As a result of this *time dilation*, people could no longer say that observers in different frames of reference would agree that two events in different places happened simultaneously. Since observers moving with respect to each other would measure time at different rates, clocks in different parts of the universe might not agree with each other. For Einstein, this was the central meaning of relativity. He called it the *relativity of simultaneity*. It meant that there is no absolute time. The fundamental properties of nature are not absolute (except for the speed of light), but relative, and their values depend on the relative motion between observers. Newtonian mechanics works well enough when objects move slowly, but it does not reflect the way the universe really operates.

Are relativistic effects real or illusory? The answer reveals the strangeness of the new relativistic universe. The effects are real to observers outside the frame of reference where they occur. If you were moving close to the speed of light in a spaceship, you would feel nothing abnormal. But if your spaceship were to collide with another body, the impact would be much greater than classical physics could predict, because with respect to the other body, your spaceship is much more massive than it seems to you.

The effects of relative time lead to several apparent paradoxes. For example, a spaceship traveling away from Earth at close to the speed of light would appear to earthbound observers to experience a slowing down of time. Not only would the spaceship's clocks appear to run slowly, but its occupants would appear to age more slowly than the people on Earth. When the spaceship returned to Earth some time later, the crew might still be very young, while those on Earth might be very old.

But if everything is relative, isn't it equally valid to say that Earth was moving away from the spaceship, and that the spaceship's crew would perceive the people on Earth to age more slowly? When the spaceship returned then, who would really have aged more slowly?

Einstein knew that as long as two reference frames are moving away from each other, both sets of observers would note the slowing of time in the other system. But to decide who had really experienced this effect, the two reference systems would have to be rejoined. The spaceship would have to return to Earth. It would have to slow down, turn around, and speed up in the opposite direction. But then it would no longer be an unaccelerated system.

Any change in speed or direction introduces an acceleration or deceleration, creating a problem outside the scope of the special theory. Einstein's theory described only uniform, or unaccelerated, frames of reference. He knew that he would eventually have to generalize the theory to take into account reference frames experiencing acceleration. This problem would occupy his thinking for the next ten years.

But he was not quite done with special relativity. In two additional papers and a review, published from November 1905 through 1907, he explored the relationship between mass and energy. He said that mass is a measure of a body's energy content. Later he came to the startling conclusion that energy and mass are interchangeable, and hence, equivalent.

In these papers, Einstein introduced his famous formula for that equivalence, $E = mc^2$. Every mass has an energy equivalent to the mass of the body multiplied by c^2, the square of the speed of light. Since the square of the speed of light is a very large number, a small unit of mass is equivalent to an enormous amount of energy.

The effect of *time dilation* can be best understood by imagining the following situation. Suppose you are standing on an embankment near a railroad track watching a single railroad car speed by. Within that railroad car, there is a person controlling a flashing lantern attached to the car's ceiling, and on the floor of the car there is a light-detecting device. The person in the car flashes the lantern and watches a beam of light travel straight down to the light-detecting device. When it hits the device, a stopclock connected to it stops one unit of time from when the beam left the lantern.

On the embankment, you too observe the light beam from the lantern. But from your perspective, the whole railroad car is moving forward rapidly, and so the beam of light moves forward as well as downward. Thus, the beam appears to travel in a diagonal path before it reaches the light detector, which is now at a new position further along the track. The diagonal path is longer than the straight path seen by the observer in the car.

Since the speed of light is constant, light must take longer to travel this diagonal path than it does to travel the vertical path. The light beam, as seen from the embankment, is not carried along or pushed forward with the added velocity of the train. It can't be, because it is already moving as fast as anything in the universe can move. For any observer, light always travels at 186,000 miles per second.

If you time the light beam from the embankment, you would find that your clock measures a slightly longer time than the clock on the train. From your point of view, events on the train take longer to happen than the observer on the train believes. Time within the train seems to have slowed down.

As the train goes faster and faster, the diagonal path of the light beam as seen from the embankment stretches out to a longer and longer distance, and the light beam appears to take longer and longer to travel that distance. Time appears to slow down even more.

When the train approaches the speed of light, the diagonal path becomes virtually parallel to the train's forward movement. The light beam would take forever to reach the floor of the car, and time would stand still. But this is all from your perspective, for the observer on the train—within the frame of reference of the light—sees nothing wrong.

At the speeds trains actually travel in our world, this time dilation is imperceptible. The light beam from the lantern in the railroad car would reach the floor when the train has moved forward by only a tiniest fraction of distance.

Train traveling at high speed

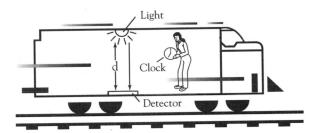

The way things appear to a person inside the train

The way things appear to a person outside the train

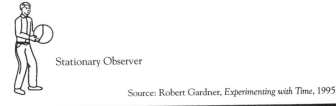

Stationary Observer

Source: Robert Gardner, *Experimenting with Time*, 1995

Scientists verified the relationship in the 1930s by comparing the energy released in a nuclear reaction to the change in mass of the nuclear particles. This new relationship between mass and energy had a tremendous impact on modern science and the world at large. Physicists came to think of mass and energy as interchangeable, of matter as a kind of congealed energy. The knowledge that a small amount of matter yields a vast amount of energy gave scientists an important clue to how the sun burns without consuming itself and how radioactive elements give off so much radiation without turning into burnt cinders.

On July 16, 1945, the enormous release of energy predicted by Einstein's equation was confirmed in the Alamogordo desert of New Mexico, where American scientists detonated the first atomic bomb.

FIVE

Growing Recognition

Recognition and fame did not come to Einstein immediately after 1905. The special theory of relativity was too bizarre, too revolutionary to gain acceptance quickly. It explained the behavior of light by violating the fundamental laws of classical mechanics, and rethinking these laws was just too drastic a step for many scientists, especially when the laws still worked well enough for everyday experience. The only change in Einstein's position was a promotion at the patent office from technical expert, third class, to technical expert, second class, in April 1906. And this promotion was unrelated to his revolutionary discoveries.

A few people, however, understood from the beginning what had happened. Max Planck was one of them. Planck, the creator of the quantum theory that Einstein had supported in his paper on the photoelectric effect, was a highly respected professor at the University of Berlin. Profoundly affected when he read volume 17 of the *Annalen der Physik*, Planck began to promote the theory of relativity at scientific conferences in Berlin. He corresponded with Einstein, and expanded on his ideas in several papers. In the summer of

*Max Planck awarded Einstein
the Planck medal in 1929.*

1906, he sent his assistant, Max von Laue, to meet with Einstein in Bern. Laue and Einstein became friends, and Laue returned to Berlin amazed that such a lively and penetrating intellect could be found in the remote recesses of the Swiss civil service.

Then in 1907, Herman Minkowski, Einstein's old mathematics teacher from the ETH, who had become a distinguished professor at Göttingen University in Germany, took up the cause of relativity and introduced a new idea. Since the measurement of time depends on the motion of the observer, Minkowski proposed that relativity demanded a fusion of the concepts of space and time. At the Eightieth Congress of German Scientists and Physicians in Cologne in September 1908, Minkowski made the famous statement, "Henceforth space by itself, and time by itself, are doomed to fade away into mere shadows, and only a kind of union of the two will preserve an independent reality."[1]

Minkowski was saying that time and space are fused in a four-dimensional "space-time;" neither space nor time is independent of the other. In four-dimensional space-time, objects move through time even when they don't move through space. As objects begin to move rapidly through the dimensions of space, their movement through the dimension of time must slow down, because no object can move through space-time faster than the speed of light.

Minkowski also pointed out that in space-time, Maxwell's equations are greatly simplified, as if they are at home there. The relativity theory, he said, reveals an electromagnetic image of the world.

Minkowski's geometrical analogy went a long way toward popularizing the theory of special relativity within the scientific community, and physicists across Europe began to pull volume 17 of the *Annalen der Physik* off their shelves and to ask themselves who this obscure Swiss patent clerk was.

One of the first to realize that Einstein was in the wrong place at the patent office was Professor Alfred Kleiner of the University of Zurich, the man who had rejected his first doctoral thesis in 1901. Kleiner advised Einstein to affiliate himself with the University of Bern as a *privatdozent*, a kind of independent lecturer who received no salary from the university but who collected fees directly from his students. This would be a first step toward full university professorship.

Einstein applied for the position by submitting his 1905 paper on relativity, but the university rejected the paper as incomprehensible. At Kleiner's urging, he applied again, and in 1908 he became a privatdozent at the University of Bern, while keeping his job at the patent office. He was free to lecture on subjects that interested him, but since his lectures were conducted very early in the morning, only a few students attended. Michele Besso was one of the few who went regularly.

In September 1909 Einstein was invited to the Eighty-First Congress of German Scientists and Physicians in Salzburg, Austria. It was his first invitation to a major scientific conference. He presented a lecture, and he met Max Planck in person for the first time. Already in touch by letter, the two men warmed to each other quickly, and the association gained Einstein the attention of many other scientists.

In the same year, the University of Zurich announced a vacancy for an associate professor of theoretical physics, and Kleiner put Einstein's name forward. But Friedrich Adler, a fellow student from Einstein's days at the ETH, had also applied for the position. Adler's father was Victor Adler, the founder of the Austrian Social Democratic party. Since most of the members of the university's governing authority were Social Democrats, it seemed likely that they would favor Adler. But when Adler discovered that he was in competition with Einstein, he withdrew his application and urged the university to accept his friend in the name of science. Adler became increasingly involved in revolutionary politics after this time, and in 1916 he was imprisoned for assassinating the Austrian prime minister as a protest against the First World War.

Thanks to Adler's withdrawal, in October 1909 Einstein resigned from the patent office after a seven-year career, left

Bern, and became an associate professor at the University of Zurich. Swiss academic authorities had finally elevated him, at the age of 30, to a position more in keeping with his talents.

Mileva loved the city of Zurich, and Albert enjoyed the atmosphere of the laboratories and the lecture halls at the university. In 1910, their second son, Eduard, was born, and in the same year Einstein's sister Maja married Paul Winteler, the son of the professor Einstein had boarded with at the Swiss Cantonal School in Aarau. Life was pleasant, yet the Einsteins stayed in Zurich only two years. Einstein was only an associate professor, which meant he had a lot of teaching responsibilities that took time away from his research. With a second son, there was also the problem of earning enough to support his family.

So, in 1911 Einstein accepted a full professorship at the German University of Prague. Planck had written to the university authorities in Prague in support of Einstein's appointment, saying, "If Einstein's theory should prove to be correct, as I expect it will, he will be considered the Copernicus of the twentieth century."[2] There was some difficulty with the appointment, because the aging emperor Franz Josef had mandated that all professors declare a religious affiliation. Einstein had long ago abandoned any belief in the tenets of organized religion, and he could be stubborn about it. But eventually he agreed to be identified as Jewish. His religion was listed, in the language of the time, as "Mosaic," and the professorship was confirmed.

Prague, then part of the Austro-Hungarian empire, was an old, beautiful city caught up in the turbulent politics of the time. Tensions raged between the German-speaking population and Czech nationalists, and caught in the middle were a large number of Jews facing a rising tide of anti-Semitism. The situation became so strained that the University of Prague, the oldest in Europe, was broken into separate Czech and German universities, whose separate faculties had little contact with each other. Einstein was to teach at the German branch.

In Prague, Einstein became aware of the growing difficulties faced by central European Jews, but he was still relatively unmoved by politics and concentrated on his teaching and his scientific work. He was not a particularly successful teacher. His lack of concern for social etiquette and his casual, even sloppy, habits of dress did not endear him to the other professors. He was more comfortable with his students, but even here he could be withdrawn at times, and his lectures were of an indifferent quality unless he was talking about a problem of interest to himself.

He made one new close friend, the Viennese professor of physics Paul Ehrenfest. Ehrenfest was an amateur pianist, and within days of meeting, the two men were playing duets, with Einstein on his violin. Einstein also made the acquaintance of the writer Franz Kafka, who at the time was working during the day for an insurance company and in his spare time just beginning to turn out the strange stories that would make him famous.

The scientific problem that preoccupied Einstein during his time in Prague was the need to generalize the relativity theory to account for accelerating reference frames, including those falling in gravity. But he was also aware of the other, unrelated problems troubling physicists at this time. There was the problem of the theory of the quantum, to which Einstein had contributed. How could energy radiate through space discontinuously, as if made up of particles, when other evidence suggested that this radiation took the form of continuous waves?

And there was the problem of the atom. The discovery of radioactive elements in 1896 had led to theories of the "decay," or breaking apart, of atoms. It was thought that radioactive atoms break into atoms of other elements, releasing electromagnetic radiation, a nonvisible form of light, as they do so. This implied that atoms are made up of smaller particles. Scientists were asking: Just what is the internal structure of the atom? What are the laws governing its decay? How does it absorb and emit the wave-particles of electromagnetic energy?

In June 1911 the Belgian industrialist Ernest Solvay sponsored a five-day conference in Brussels to discuss these problems. In the hope of generating new ideas, Solvay paid the expenses for Europe's greatest scientific minds to come to the conference. There were twenty-one participants. Einstein was of course one of them, as were Max Planck, Hendrik Lorentz, Henri Poincare, Marie Curie, and Ernest Rutherford.

Known as the First Solvay Conference, it sparked intense discussions but produced no solutions. For Einstein, however, the conference was a final recognition that he was a full member of Europe's small circle of leading theoretical physicists. In fact, Planck was so impressed with Einstein that upon returning to Berlin, he and the chemist Hermann Walther Nernst began thinking of ways to bring him back to Germany.

Einstein did not stay long in Prague. Now that he was well known in the European scientific community, his services were in demand. He received offers to teach from universities in Vienna, Utrecht, and Leiden, but the offer that intrigued him most came from his alma mater, by now called the ETH, in Zurich, where he had failed to obtain a post after graduation. Mileva was uncomfortable in Prague and welcomed the opportunity to return to Zurich. In October 1912 the Einsteins were back in Zurich and Albert was teaching at the ETH.

But his third stay in Zurich lasted only two years. In the early summer of 1913, Planck and Nernst traveled down from Berlin to meet with Einstein in his offices at the ETH. They made him an extraordinary offer. If he would agree to return to Germany, they would petition the Ministry of Education to make him director of the forthcoming Kaiser Wilhelm Institute for Physics, a full professor at the University of Berlin, and a member of the Royal Prussian Academy of Sciences, with a special stipend in excess of anything he had earned before. None of these positions would require any teaching. He would be free to do pure research, yet he could

The First Solvay Conference in 1911 brought together the leading scientists of Europe, including Einstein, standing second from right. Max Planck is standing second from left; Hendrik Lorentz is seated fourth from the left; and Marie Curie is seated second from the right.

teach whenever he wished. Furthermore, no questions would arise over his renunciation of German citizenship or his religion.

Einstein asked for a few hours to decide, during which the two Berlin professors went for an excursion in the nearby mountains. Einstein had few pleasant memories of Germany and he knew that Prussian autocracy was stronger than ever.

But here was an opportunity to provide adequately for his family, to do theoretical work without other responsibilities, and to associate with the physics department of the University of Berlin—in all of Europe rivaled only by Cambridge's Cavendish Laboratory. When Planck and Nernst returned from the mountains, Einstein told them he would accept the appointment.

Anxious to promote the nation's technological development by acquiring the most promising scientific thinkers, the German Ministry of Education granted Einstein everything Planck and Nernst offered. For some years afterward, there was confusion over the issue of his citizenship. Einstein always claimed that he had insisted on keeping his Swiss citizenship, though German authorities ingeniously claimed that membership in the Royal Prussian Academy automatically renewed Einstein's German citizenship. But the issue did not get in the way of the approval of Einstein's appointment by Kaiser Wilhelm II in November 1913.

In April 1914 the Einsteins moved to Berlin. Einstein's marriage ended a short time later. Mileva took the two boys back to Zurich and never returned. The relationship had been deteriorating for some time, and the separation came as a relief to Einstein.

Four months after Einstein's arrival in Berlin, the growing tensions between the European powers exploded into world war. Conflict in the Balkans had intensified as various groups of Slavic nationalists sought to separate themselves from the Austro-Hungarian empire. Germany supported Austria's efforts to suppress the uprisings. The Russians supported the Slavs, and England and France soon followed suit. When on June 28, 1914, a Bosnian Serb revolutionary assassinated the Austrian Archduke, the heir to the throne, the Russian army mobilized along its borders, and Austria declared war on Serbia. In early August, Germany launched a massive invasion of France through neutral Belgium. Europe was plunged into four years of bloody trench warfare and massive slaughter on a scale unimagined by any of the statesmen and generals.

Einstein watched in quiet horror as the European scientific community disintegrated. Travel restrictions, rules of secrecy, and the militarization of scientific research made cooperative relations and the sharing of information difficult. Succumbing to patriotic fervor and national chauvinism, scientists in all the belligerent countries were drawn into war work. In Berlin Einstein witnessed his friend, the chemist Fritz Haber, and Walther Nernst join forces to create the German chemical warfare industry. The two men supervised the production of chlorine and mustard gas to be used as weapons on the battlefronts. Scientists of different nationalities who only months before had sat together and shared their ideas at conferences now became the most bitter of enemies.

All this disturbed Einstein greatly, and his instinctive hatred of militarism now evolved into a full-blown pacifism. In the international press, Germany was characterized as an aggressor nation for its invasion of neutral Belgium, and it was charged that militarism dominated German culture. German intellectuals began to feel that the world hated them.

In October 1914, ninety-three leading German intellectuals, including Max Planck, William Roentgen, and the biologist Paul Ehrlich, signed a "Manifesto to the Civilized World" that denied German responsibility for starting the war and proclaimed that "German culture and German militarism are identical." Einstein not only refused to sign, but he and the University of Berlin physiology professor George Nicolai wrote a dissenting document known as the "Manifesto to Europeans." It denounced nationalist passions and called upon all Europeans to think of themselves as members of one culture, with common interests transcending those of the warring governments. Aside from Einstein and Nicolai, only two others were courageous enough to sign the protest.

For a time, Einstein became involved in the Bund Neues Vaterland, a small group agitating for an early peace. The

Bund was outlawed in February 1916, and only Einstein's stature and his Swiss citizenship prevented him from running afoul of the imperial German government.

After Mileva and his sons left him, Einstein found himself spending more time with a distant cousin, Elsa Lowenthal, for whom he had developed a strong attraction as early as 1912.

Elsa was a recent divorcee with two daughters, Ilse and Margot. During the war years, Einstein suffered from stomach trouble, and he found in Elsa a willing and attentive nurse. The material comforts of her household provided a refuge from the war hysteria, and in a nation increasingly obsessed with food rationing, he was well taken care of. Still, he did not fully recover his health until 1920.

He sent money to Mileva and his sons in Zurich, though this became harder to do as the war went on. He tried to visit the boys in Zurich when he could. On one such visit to Switzerland in September 1915, he went to Vevey on Lake Geneva to meet with the writer and pacifist Romain Rolland, to whom he confessed his disgust for the martial spirit of the German character and the failure of German intellectuals to resist the war. Some friends urged him to stay in neutral Switzerland, but he returned to Berlin and buried himself in his theoretical work, all the time hoping for a German defeat.

The war finally ended in November 1918 with the exhaustion and surrender of Germany. The face of Europe changed radically. The Kaiser abdicated and the Prussian generals relinquished control of the country to a new government later known as the Weimar Republic. In Russia, the Romanov dynasty had been dethroned by revolution the year before, and Lenin was now building a socialist state. The Austro-Hungarian empire also collapsed, replaced by new Austrian, Hungarian, and Czechoslovak states.

Einstein was pleased with the German defeat and the emergence of republican government, but over the next few years the enormous sums of money demanded by France and

Einstein's cousin Elsa in her home in Berlin

England as war reparations kept the German economy weak. In spite of the armistice, Germany was still subject to an Allied blockade in certain areas of international trade. Inflation rendered people's wages worthless as the government printed more and more money to cope with its problems. Obtaining food was difficult, and starvation was a real threat.

The ranks of the unemployed provided recruits for extremist political movements of both the Right and the Left. Revolutionary workers and students wanted more radical changes, and clashed in the streets with embittered nationalists who blamed the new government's civilian leaders for the nation's defeat. The new German republic remained very fragile. Einstein was also troubled by the fact that in the years right after the war German scientists, with himself as an exception, were not invited to the Solvay conferences.

In 1919 Einstein's divorce from Mileva became official, and he married his cousin Elsa. With most of his energies devoted to complex scientific problems, Einstein was often quite helpless in domestic affairs and in dealing with the public demands placed on a famous man. Elsa understood his need for privacy and in the years to come would try to protect him from the constant stream of people seeking his attention. These efforts were a continuation of those during the war years, when she provided him with a secure environment to pursue the unsolved problems of general relativity.

SIX

THE GENERAL THEORY

While the war raged around him, Einstein struggled with the problem of nonuniform, or accelerated, motion. Why is it so different from uniform motion? Specifically, why can an observer detect the nonuniform motion of his or her frame of reference, but not its uniform motion? In a very smooth-riding car, we may not be able to tell whether we are stopped or moving at a steady speed if we are not looking out the window. But when a car speeds up or slows down, we don't have to look out the window to sense the change. We feel it inside our bodies as our mass resists the acceleration. If the change is abrupt, loose objects fly about, indicating the change in motion. If the vehicle turns, our bodies want to continue going straight, moving toward the side of the vehicle. How could the principle of relativity be generalized to include nonuniform motion?

In the real universe, Einstein could see, most motion is not uniform, but accelerated. The planets in their orbits continually change direction and speed. Wherever there is a gravitational field, the objects within it are being accelerated, and gravitational fields exist wherever there are material objects. Einstein began to look closely at the properties of both acceleration and gravity.

Newton had described these phenomena in two separate laws—the second law of motion and the universal law of gravitation. The second law of motion says that the more massive an object is, the smaller the acceleration a given force will produce. That's because mass resists being pulled by a force, a property called *inertia*. The gravitational law says that the greater the masses of two objects, the greater the force of attraction between them. In one case, mass resists acceleration, and in the other, mass increases gravitation. It suggested to Newton that there are two kinds of mass. To Einstein, this did not make sense.

Newton saw no contradiction. In fact, he used the opposing effects of mass to explain why all objects fall to Earth at the same acceleration, no matter what their mass. But Einstein could not believe that there was an inertial mass that obeyed one set of laws, and a gravitational mass that obeyed another set of laws.

As he explored the connection between acceleration and gravitation, Einstein began to see that accelerated motion could be relative, just as uniform motion between two reference frames is relative. An object that is accelerating in one frame of reference could be motionless in a gravitational field in another (see box on p. 66.) This *principle of equivalence* between gravity and acceleration was the foundation stone of the general theory of relativity. It led to the odd conclusion that gravity causes light to bend.

After announcing the principle of equivalence in 1907, Einstein in 1911 predicted that the bending of light in a strong gravitational field such as the Sun's should be detectable during a solar eclipse. He reasoned that the rays of light coming toward us from stars behind the Sun should be bent slightly, creating the impression that those stars had a different position in the sky from the position they occupied when the Sun wasn't in the way.

German scientists, under Professor Erwin Freundlich of the

Suppose an observer were inside a box so far away from Earth that its gravitational field had no influence. What would happen if this box were accelerated upward, increasing its speed by approximately 32 feet per second every second (9.8 m/s²)—the rate of acceleration caused by gravity on the surface of Earth?

The resistance of the observer's inertial mass to the acceleration would push him against the floor of the box with a force equal to that of Earth's gravity. Looking at it another way, the floor of the box would push up against the feet of the observer with a force equal to that of Earth's

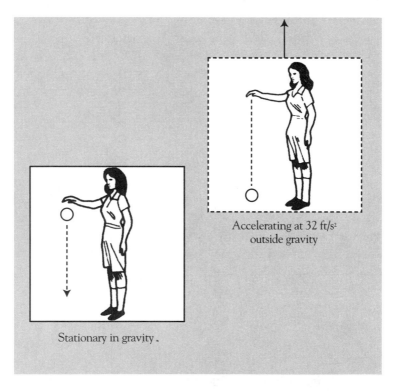

Accelerating at 32 ft/s²
outside gravity

Stationary in gravity.

Figure 3. A person being accelerated at the rate of gravity in outer space would have the equivalent experience of a person who is motionless in Earth's gravity.

gravity. Unless the observer could look outside the box, she would have no way of telling whether the box was accelerating or resting on the surface of Earth. An object undergoing acceleration, Einstein concluded, could not be distinguished from an object embedded in a gravitational field, except by an observer in another frame of reference. Einstein called this idea the principle of equivalence between acceleration and gravity.

The principle of equivalence implied that within a nonuniform frame of reference or system, no experiment should be able to distinguish whether the system is accelerating or being pulled by the force of gravity. An observer inside an accelerating car could detect the acceleration by watching a light beam travel vertically from the ceiling to the floor of the car. Since light cannot accelerate with the car, the beam would appear to the observer to curve backward, completely missing a detector on the floor.

For the principle of equivalence to hold, for acceleration to be indistinguishable from gravity, light also had to bend in a gravitational field. If the gravitational field was strong enough, all the relativistic effects in time and space of an object accelerating at a very high speed should be detectable.

Berlin University Observatory, planned to test Einstein's prediction by making observations of a solar eclipse in southern Russia in the summer of 1914. But World War I intervened. The German scientists were in Russia at the outbreak of hostilities and became prisoners of war.

Curved Space

The idea that beams of light, which have no mass, could be bent by a gravitational force contradicted Newton's idea that gravity is a force of attraction between material objects. But Einstein had shown that energy and mass are interchangeable. Light consists of energy, and therefore possesses mass in

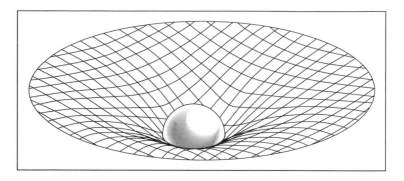

Figure 4. Einstein found that space curves around massive objects.

an altered form. Taking this into account, the bending of light does not seem so strange. In the years after 1911, Einstein took his boldest leap of imagination yet, and began looking at the problem in an entirely different way. To do so, he brought together the mathematics of Minkowski and his notion of four-dimensional space-time, the notion of force as a field of influence rather than as something capable of acting on an object from a distance, and the work of the German mathematician Georg Friedrich Riemann.

In the 1850s, Riemann had worked out a new system of geometry based on curved surfaces, as opposed to plane geometry. It was Einstein's old friend Marcel Grossman who brought to his attention Riemann's geometry and a sophisticated branch of mathematics known as *tensor calculus* that could be used to describe curvature in space-time. Einstein began to think of his curving light rays not as influenced by a gravitational force, but as traveling through a space that was somehow curved. Just as a golf ball rolls right or left over the contours of a hilly green, just as a locomotive on a curved track must follow the rails, light beams follow curved paths, or bends, in space-time.

Those bends occur wherever matter is present. A small amount of matter causes almost undetectable bending, but a massive object causes a significant curvature in space. Wherever there is a curvature, light and all material objects are restricted to move along it.

At the heart of the general theory of relativity was Einstein's assertion that gravity is not a force, but a property of the geometry of space. The planets orbit the Sun because the Sun's huge mass curves the space in its vicinity, and the planets circle like marbles caught in invisible grooves. The general theory of relativity is, in essense, a new theory of gravitation.

Einstein verified the theory for himself when in 1915 he used it to explain a phenomenon that did not fit within Newton's theory. It was the strange orbit of the planet Mercury. Not only does Mercury revolve around the Sun along an elliptical path, but the ellipse itself moves gradually around the Sun too. In other words, the closest point of travel to the Sun, the *perihelion*, shifts slightly with each revolution; it precesses. Newton's theory of gravitation could not explain this motion, but the theory of general relativity could. Relativity suggests that a planet would spin in the gravitational "well" of curved space near the Sun's mass, causing its orbit to precess. All the planets have this precession, but it is large enough to detect only when the orbit is very elliptical, as is the case with the inner planets like Mercury.

When Einstein saw that calculations based on his theory so clearly agreed with Mercury's orbit, he was certain the theory had to be right. His heart began palpitating, and he could not work for three days because of his excitement. Later he said he felt that something had snapped in him at that moment. It may have been the most emotional event of his career.

One week later Einstein presented the final version of his theory. He completed his first systematic summary of the whole theory for volume 49 of the *Annalen der Physik* in March 1916 in a paper entitled "The Foundations of the General Theory of Relativity." A popular presentation was published in book form the following year under the title *Relativity: The Special and the General Theory.*

The next step was to try once again to verify Einstein's prediction of the bending of starlight during an eclipse. The inability to study the eclipse near the start of the war was a blessing in disguise for Einstein. His original prediction was made before he incorporated the mathematics of curved space. When he revised the calculation in 1915, the deflection of starlight increased by a factor of 2.

In spite of wartime restrictions, Einstein was able to communicate with the Dutch physicist Hendrik Lorentz and the astronomer Willem de Sitter in neutral Holland. De Sitter passed a copy of volume 49 of the *Annalen der Physik* on to the English astronomer Arthur Eddington. Eddington was a Quaker and a pacifist who had no use for the war or the way it distorted relations with foreign scientists, and he recognized right away the importance of Einstein's work. He and the British Astronomer Royal, Frank Dyson, began to make plans for the necessary observations during a solar eclipse that was to occur on May 29, 1919. About six months after the end of the war, two teams were sent to Sobral, Brazil, and to the island of Principe on the west coast of Africa, locations where the eclipse would be total.

On November 6, 1919, at a special joint meeting of the Royal Society and the Royal Astronomical Society in London, the results of the eclipse expedition were announced. They confirmed Einstein's prediction for the bending of starlight. The British astronomers and physicists were clearly aware of what had happened. The day after the meeting, on November 7, 1919, the *London Times* announced the confirmation of general relativity under the headline "Revolution in Science. Newtonian Ideas Overthrown."

Other predictions of the theory have since proved accurate. The theory says that the gravitational field of a massive object like a star pulls on the light leaving its surface, stealing its energy by stretching out its wavelength and decreasing its frequency. When such starlight is examined through a prism, its spectrum should be redder than expected. This effect, known as a *redshift,* was eventually confirmed. Other more

Einstein's theory of relativity was confirmed when scientists made observations during a solar eclipse. Scientists who played a part include Paul Ehrenfest, standing to the right of Einstein; Willem de Sitter, standing to the far right; Arthur Eddington, sitting on the left; and Hendrik Lorentz sitting on the right.

bizarre effects, such as clocks ticking more slowly in strong gravitational fields, have been confirmed in modern times.

Acceptance of general relativity meant a reorganization of scientific thought on a scale not seen for more than two hundred years, when Galileo and Newton turned the world from medieval mysticism and set it on its mechanistic course. Newton, revolutionary genius though he was, had not seen a complete picture of that universe. The mathematics that support his laws of motion and his law of gravitational attraction work with great accuracy in everyday experience, but where speeds are very high, the mathematics are inadequate. Reality is stranger than it appears, and it is more precisely described by Einstein's mathematics and geometrical imagery. A profound and revolutionary law of nature had been proven, a second scientific revolution had been initiated, and a new scientific genius had been crowned.

J. J. Thompson, discoverer of the electron and then president of the Royal Society, spoke of the general theory of relativity as "one of the greatest—perhaps the greatest—of achievements in the history of human thought."[1] Eddington, aware of the irony of British scientists confirming a theory developed by their former enemies, wrote to Einstein and called the announced results "the best possible thing that could have happened for scientific relations between England and Germany."[2]

Thus, Einstein emerged from the small, closed world of university laboratories and scientific conferences to become a figure of international prominence.

SEVEN

A RISING STAR

After the eclipse expedition confirmed general relativity in 1919, Einstein experienced a meteoric rise to world fame. His ascent was incredibly rapid and widespread, in part because it was the first major scientific revolution to occur in an age of mass communications and mass education. Another factor was that in the aftermath of war, people's faith in rigid values collapsed, and philosophers, artists, and other European intellectuals became attracted to any idea that undermined the certainty of knowledge.

Einstein's own personality played a part in his fame. Modest and totally lacking in pretension, he could be very charming. Obsessed with the deepest problems of physics, he could not be bothered with how he dressed, and he was often forgetful about simple things. This genius of science had a profoundly simple, almost childlike nature, and he endeared himself to a world public as the perfect image of the absentminded professor. Even to Germany's former enemies, he was the German it was impossible to hate.

Fame brought Einstein mail by the sackful, a constant stream of journalists begging for interviews, and invitations

Einstein was popular with journalists and the public.

from universities and scientific societies all over the world to visit and lecture on relativity. He was willing to popularize the theory of relativity, but he regarded all the hero worship with amusement.

All the same, in the years that followed he traveled widely and endeavored to fulfill many of the requests, for he had come to see himself in a different light. He knew that his reputation as a scientific genius and as a German who had opposed the war could be exploited to heal old wounds, to help restore international scientific cooperation, and to promote the causes of world peace and democratic political reform within Germany. As he became a public figure whose every remark was widely reported in the press, he emerged from the world of science and readily lent his support to what he regarded as worthy causes—pacifism, democratic socialism, the reform of the German political and educational systems, the welfare of the European Jews, and the free flow of scientific information. He attracted many individuals and groups who wanted his support or who asked for the great man's opinion on some question of religion or philosophy.

On the other hand, while his world fame grew, within Germany there arose an increasingly vicious opposition to Einstein. Some scientists could not understand or accept relativity and resented the acclaim Einstein received for what they felt was a false theory.

Others, rightists and ultra-nationalists embittered by Germany's defeat, blamed the liberals and pacifists for the nation's humiliation, and Einstein became the focus of their hatred. Anti-Semitism was a growing element within the radical right, and Einstein was portrayed not as a German or a Swiss, but as a Jew and a socialist, and as such responsible for all of Germany's failures. His work was characterized as "degenerate Jewish science" or "Bolshevism in physics." As one German magazine put it, "In the last analysis, one cannot blame workers for being taken in by Marx, when German professors allow themselves to be misled by Einstein."[1]

In June 1920 Einstein's mother died. She had been ill for

some time, and during the war she had come to Berlin from Milan to spend her last days with her son. Soon after her death, the attacks on Einstein began in earnest. On August 27, a mass meeting was held in the Berlin Philharmonic Hall by the Study Group of German Natural Philosphers, an anti-Semitic group Einstein dubbed the "Antirelativity Company." Einstein himself sat in the audience and was much amused by the speeches. It became clear to him that no scientific arguments were being made and that his theory was being attacked as alien to German science and culture.

In late September 1920, the annual meeting of the Congress of German Scientists and Physicians was to be held in the resort spa of Bad Nauheim, near Frankfurt. A session on relativity was widely anticipated to be a confrontation between Einstein and his detractors. Since anti-Semitism and right-wing agitation were on the rise, the Weimar government feared trouble. When the delegates arrived, they found the meeting hall guarded by police with fixed bayonets.

Scheduled to speak was Philipp Lenard, the man who had conducted the experiments with the photoelectric effect that had led Einstein to propose the quantum nature of light. Lenard was an early admirer of Einstein, though he harbored some resentment that a mere theoretician, rather than an experimenter, could gain so much attention.

Lenard was one of the intellectuals who wholeheartedly supported German militarism during the war, and the defeat brought a confusion and bitterness that pushed him toward anti-Semitism, fascism, and hatred of foreigners. In his laboratory in Heidelberg, Lenard forbade the use of the word *ampere* for units of electrical current because it was derived from the name of a French scientist.

Fortunately, Lenard behaved with restraint at the conference, and the debate with Einstein remained on a scientific and philosophical level. But it was clear to many of the participants that something irrational had captured the German psyche, and there was a real fear that it would induce Einstein to leave Germany. At this point, any university in the world would have been happy to have him. Planck and others were appalled at the attacks on Einstein and begged him to remain in Germany. Einstein himself felt that for a man of his stature to leave now would irreparably damage the fragile republican government, and he decided to stick it out.

In the spring of 1921 Einstein made his first trip to the United States in the company of Chaim Weitzmann. Weitzmann, a professor of chemistry at the University of Manchester, England, had become the acknowledged leader of the Zionist movement. Zionism was a movement to establish in Palestine a Jewish homeland, a place where European Jews could resettle to escape prejudice.

As anti-Semitic incidents increased, many Jews were drawn to the Zionist cause. In view of the situation in Germany, Einstein was sympathetic to the plight of European Jews and he lent his support to Zionism. Einstein toured the United States with Weitzmann, using his prestige to raise money for the Zionists and ultimately for a new Hebrew University to be built in Jerusalem.

If Einstein had been puzzled and amused by the adulation heaped upon him in Europe, he was positively overwhelmed by his reception in America. When the Weitzmanns and the Einsteins arrived in New York aboard the *Rotterdam* on April 2, 1921, reporters mobbed the ship. Einstein stood on deck, a briar pipe in one hand and his violin case in the other, answering an endless stream of questions.

Asked to explain relativity in just a few sentences, he gamely responded, "It was formerly believed that if all material things disappeared out of the universe, time and space would be left. According to the relativity theory, however, time and space disappear together with the things." Elsa was asked if she understood her husband's theory. She said no, but "it is not necessary to my happiness." Weitzmann himself facetiously remarked that on the voyage Einstein "explained his theory to me every day and on my arrival I was fully convinced that he understood it."[2]

Journalists followed Einstein wherever he went, and the

experience left him with a reluctance to give interviews. Jewish supporters and crowds of the curious gathered around him, and everyone who was anyone wanted to meet him. He was honored by the mayor of New York and President Warren G. Harding. With Einstein as the star attraction, the group raised a modest amount of money for the Zionist cause.

Einstein lectured on relativity at Columbia University and Princeton University. The four Princeton lectures were published in a book titled *The Meaning of Relativity*. While Einstein was at Princeton, word came of an experiment conducted by the American physicist Dayton Clarence Miller in which he claimed the ether had been detected, supposedly invalidating fifteen years of Einstein's work. With supreme confidence that Miller had erred, Einstein responded to the news with a famous statement that reflected both his faith in the beauty of his theory and his personal conception of the underlying logic of nature's laws. "Subtle is the Lord, but malicious He is not."[3] In 1930, the phrase was carved into the marble fireplace in the faculty lounge of Princeton's new mathematics and physics building.

When he returned from the United States in June 1921, Einstein briefly visited England as a guest of the British statesman Viscount R. B. Haldane. It was something of a risk for both men, because feelings still ran high against the Germans in England. But Einstein's naturalness, warmth, and humor charmed his audiences. He lectured at Manchester and London Universities and was introduced to many prominent personalities, including the philosopher Alfred North Whitehead and the playwright George Bernard Shaw. He visited Westminster Abbey and laid a wreath at the tomb of Isaac Newton.

British scientists, on the whole, were committed experimentalists, and tended to look askance at a theory like Einstein's that seemed the product of pure theoretical speculation, even though their own experiments had confirmed the theory. They regarded German science as somewhat mystical, but after Einstein's lectures they began

78

President Warren G. Harding (center) was one of many people who wanted to meet Einstein on his trip to the United States in 1921.

to see the logic behind the theory and the genius behind the man.

A visit to Paris followed in the spring of 1922, where Einstein was asked to join the Committee on Intellectual Cooperation of the newly formed League of Nations. The victorious nations were keeping Germany out of the league, and German nationalists feared its intentions. As a result, the situation was very delicate politically for Einstein.

Einstein joined the committee, though he was uncertain what it could accomplish. He had strong reservations about the League's power to mediate international conflicts. In early 1923, French troops occupied the Ruhr valley in Germany's industrial heartland in order to force the nation to continue paying its war debts. When the League proved unable to act against this aggression, Einstein resigned from the committee. He was later pressured into joining again, but his relationship with the League of Nations was ambivalent until he finally cut his ties in 1932.

The situation in Germany continued to deteriorate. On June 24, 1922, Walther Rathenau, the foreign minister of the Weimar Republic and a friend of Einstein's, was assassinated by right-wing extremists. Since Rathenau was Jewish, and had just established diplomatic relations with the new Bolshevik Soviet state, he was the perfect target for the extremists. At the time, extremist elements were gathering around the National Socialist German Workers' Party, led since 1921 by the Austrian war veteran Adolf Hitler.

When Rathenau was killed, Einstein again contemplated leaving Germany. His colleagues talked him out of it, believing that his presence in Germany gave a symbolic boost to the forces of reform. But Einstein had received threats. There was real concern that he would also be a target for assassination. He was Germany's most prominent Jewish scientist, an advocate of pacifism and internationalism, and a supporter of liberal and socialist causes. He began to wonder how much longer Berlin would provide a comfortable working environment.

In October 1922 the Einsteins embarked on a tour of Japan and the Far East. In Japan he was received by the Emperor and Empress, and he gave several lectures on relativity to attentive audiences who patiently sat through long translations from German into Japanese.

In Japan Einstein learned that he had been awarded the 1921 Nobel Prize "for his services to theoretical physics and in particular for his discovery of the law of the photoelectric effect." The Royal Swedish Academy of Sciences avoided any mention of the theory of relativity. Though the theory had been experimentally verified, it was still controversial— and for many people, simply incomprehensible.

The Academy also had to consider its own rule that a prize-winning discovery had to be of some practical benefit to humankind. In the 1920s, the theory of relativity seemed to have little practical application. So Einstein was instead given the Nobel Prize for his work in developing the theory of the quantum.

Unable to attend the award ceremony in Sweden, the German ambassador to Sweden accepted the prize for him. This created a minor incident, for the Swiss also claimed Einstein as a citizen and wanted their ambassador to accept the award. Einstein concurred that he was a Swiss citizen and expressed the desire to have the Swiss ambassador to Germany present him with the medal when he returned to Berlin. In the end, however, it was the Swedish ambassador to Germany who presented the medal to him.

The Einsteins continued their tour through Shanghai, Hong Kong, and Singapore, and before returning to Europe they stopped in Palestine. Here Einstein gave the inaugural address at the opening of the first buildings of the new Hebrew University in Jerusalem. From Palestine they traveled to Spain, returning to Berlin in the spring of 1923.

It was not until July 1923 that Einstein was able to travel to Goteborg, Sweden, to give his delayed acceptance speech for the Nobel Prize. He ignored the language of the citation and lectured on relativity. In keeping with a promise Einstein

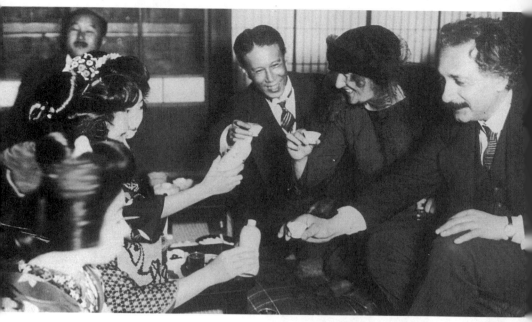

Top: Albert and Elsa visited Japan in a tour of the Far East in 1922. Bottom: Einstein in the Einstein Tower in Potsdam, Germany.

had made as part of his divorce settlement, the prize money, about $32,000, went to Mileva and his two sons.

In 1924 the leader of the abortive German eclipse expedition, now calling himself Erwin Finlay-Freundlich, opened the Einstein Institute in Potsdam, Germany. The institute was actually a new observatory designed to detect the redshift in starlight predicted by the general theory of relativity. Its special telescope was housed in the "Einstein Tower," a boldly curved building of white concrete, designed by Erich Mendelsohn, that reflected revolutionary trends in modern German architecture.

The building became one of Potsdam's tourist attractions, but its very modernism and its association with Einstein's "Jewish" theories made it a target for fascists. The Fascist Party, which had taken power in Italy under Benito Mussolini while the Einsteins were in the Far East, denounced all of modern art as "degenerate."

In May 1925 the Einsteins traveled to South America, where they visited Brazil, Uruguay, and Argentina. Upon returning to Berlin in June, Einstein tried to take life at a slower pace. He gave lectures at the University of Berlin and as a visiting professor at the University of Leiden in Holland. Occasionally he would take trips to visit his sons in Zurich, where he could relax in the atmosphere of a city he had loved since his student days.

EIGHT

FROM RADICAL TO CONSERVATIVE

Despite the political turmoil, Berlin still provided Einstein a certain degree of comfort and security for his scientific work, which now centered on two problems. Einstein had noted striking similarities between his equations describing the geometry of a gravitational field and Maxwell's equations describing electromagnetic fields. He thought it might be possible to find one set of equations to describe both gravity and electromagnetism, proving them to be different aspects of one fundamental force of nature. Maxwell had shown that electricity and magnetism were really a single force, and now Einstein wanted to apply the same process of unification to all the known forces.

Other scientists had already begun to search for a *unified field theory*. Einstein would labor on this problem for the rest of his life, rejecting one set of mathematical constructs after another. He never found the answer, and to date, no one else has. Modern physicists believe they have the outlines of a unified field theory embracing electromagnetism and two forces within atomic nuclei, but the relationship of gravity to these three forces eludes them. Some physicists now doubt that a unified field theory is possible. It remains one of the great undecided questions of modern physics.

Einstein's other concern was the direction taken by the quantum theory in the years since he had said that energy travels in particlelike packets instead of continuous waves. Here he and Planck, after starting the quantum revolution, became the scientific conservatives, watching from the sidelines as younger scientists proposed a number of very bizarre ideas.

These ideas began with attempts to explain how atoms give off radiation. In 1911 the English physicist Ernest Rutherford had proposed that an atom contains a tightly packed nucleus of positively charged protons at its center, with a swarm of negatively charged electrons orbiting around the nucleus some distance away. Physicists accepted Rutherford's model of the atom, but the stability of the orbiting electrons was hard to explain, considering that atoms give off radiation, or electromagnetic energy. Since they lose energy, the electron orbits should eventually be pulled into the nucleus. Thus the structure of the atom should collapse.

In 1913 the brilliant young Danish physicist Neils Bohr gave a better picture of the atom's structure. He suggested that it is better to think of electron orbits as energy levels—"slots" in which electrons remain until they absorb or release energy. If an electron is hit by just the right size quantum of energy, say a photon of light, it absorbs that quantum and jumps to a higher energy level, or orbit. The electron is then said to be in an "excited" state.

The electron eventually returns to its normal energy level, in the process giving off a quantum of energy of the same size it had absorbed. Not all imaginable energy levels are permitted by nature, just as not all sizes of quanta are absorbed and emitted; the energy levels increase in a stepwise fashion. The beauty of this new theory is in the way it describes a perfect correspondence between electron orbital shifts and the

Einstein with physicist Neils Bohr

emission or absorption of matching quanta of energy. The quantum jumps of the electrons maintain the energy balance of the atom and explain its stability.

Einstein embraced this aspect of quantum theory. In 1916 he wrote an important paper suggesting that a gas of atoms could be induced to emit photons. This process, known as *stimulated emission*, has in our own time led to the development of the laser.

On the subatomic level, Bohr's ideas were beginning to undermine those of classical mechanics, leading the way to the new science of quantum mechanics. Around the nucleus of the Bohr atom swarmed a cloud of electrons whose random jumps to different orbits release the little bundles of energy Einstein had discovered in light. Bohr had answered the questions about the structure and behavior of the atom raised by the First Solvay Congress in 1911. The joining of the Rutherford atom to quantum theory earned Bohr the Nobel Prize in 1922, and Denmark made him director of a new Institute for Theoretical Physics in Copenhagen. Einstein himself called Bohr's work "the highest form of musicality in the sphere of thought."[1]

Bohr's work, however, would take physics in a new direction that Einstein found hard to accept. It became apparent that no scientific law could predict exactly when an individual electron would give off a photon and drop to a less energetic orbit. The quantum jump seemed to be a purely spontaneous process, like the decay of radioactive atoms. The release of an individual quantum of energy at any point in time could be probable, but never certain. In the realm of the very small, the laws of chance seemed to rule.

It was not long before the German physicist Werner Heisenberg announced his *uncertainty principle* (see box on p. 88), in which he said that a particle's position and momentum could not be determined with absolute certainty. An investigator could measure one of the two quantities with reasonable certainty, but would have to sacrifice certainty of

In 1923 the French physicist Louis de Broglie, using Einstein's idea that mass and energy are equivalent, proposed that material particles such as electrons sometime behave like particles and sometime like waves. De Broglie's *matter-waves* extended the notion of wave-particle duality from light to material objects. He envisioned both photons and electrons as particles guided by waves.

After reading about de Broglie's matter-waves in the footnote of one of Einstein's papers, the Austrian physicist Erwin Schrödinger practically dispensed with the notion of an electron as a particle altogether in 1924. He developed equations describing the electron's movement in terms of "wave mechanics." Quantum mechanics was born. Einstein admired and publicized the work of de Broglie and Schrödinger, but had difficulty with the strange developments that came next.

In 1926 the German physicist Max Born suggested that matter-waves are nothing more than waves of probability that an electron exists at a particular point. Where the waves cancel each other out, the probability is very low that an electron exists at that point; where the waves reinforce each other, the probability is strong that an electron could be detected there.

The German physicist Werner Heisenberg had a critical insight as a result of this view. He realized that the process of making scientific measurements must affect the ultimate position of each particle. To get information about an entity, a scientist has to illuminate it with light or some other form of energy and observe the reflected light. But the energy itself affects the entity and may alter the very

the other quantity in return. Einstein, revolutionary thinker though he was, could not accept the idea that the behavior of a particle could not be predicted from one point in time to another. He objected to a universe that, at whatever level, information the scientist is after. The electron is such a tiny object that a photon of light can alter its position and momentum significantly.

Heisenberg announced his uncertainty principle in 1927. It says that it is impossible to know precisely both a particle's position and momentum at one point in time. One of these values can be determined with reasonable certainty, but not both; the certainty of one value is gained at the expense of the certainty of the other value.

Neils Bohr interpreted the uncertainty principle to mean that the uncertainty is inherent in nature. In the realm of the very small, a particle is sometimes here and sometimes not quite here, according to chance. The particle exists only as a kind of blur of probability waves until experimental detection fixes its position and momentum, always with a small degree of uncertainty. It is as if the particle cannot decide exactly where it is or how it is moving until asked.

If you can't precisely measure both position and momentum at one instant, then you can't predict with certainty how a particle will behave at the next instant. The future is only probable, not certain. This became known as the "Copenhagen interpretation" of quantum mechanics, named for the school of thought that came out of Bohr's Copenhagen Institute.

Bohr also introduced the principle of complementarity, in which he said the wave and particle aspects of light are not contradictory, but complementary. They are simply the result of using different methods to measure light. What is more, he said, it is not possible to decide the question of whether light is a wave or a particle.

was governed by statistical probabilities. He also disagreed with Bohr's idea that we can never know the true nature of light, but must accept its wave and particle characteristics as complementary.

Einstein raised his objections to quantum mechanics at the

Fifth Solvay Congress held in Belgium in October 1927. Einstein and Bohr, who had great respect and admiration for each other, engaged in a lively debate over the uncertainty principle. Einstein thought of one experiment after another to measure position and momentum at the same instant, but in each case Bohr found a logical flaw. In exasperation, Einstein said, "God does not play dice with the universe." But Bohr insisted that it is so. Einstein remained unconvinced, believing that the quantum mechanics explanation was incomplete.

For the rest of his life, Einstein insisted that the uncertainty of quantum theory would yield to a more deterministic theory. But quantum theory endured, and a younger generation of scientists came to think of Einstein, in spite of his world fame, as stubbornly old-fashioned—even irrelevant. The process of raising objections to Bohr's views, however, helped to sharpen the debate over quantum theory and to force its supporters to work harder at confirming it.

In 1928, returning from a lecture tour in Switzerland, Einstein collapsed while trying to carry his heavy suitcase across the snow-covered platform of a Swiss railway station. His doctors diagnosed heart trouble. To ease the burden on her famous husband, Elsa hired a young woman, Helen Dukas, to work as his secretary. Dukas stayed with Einstein for the rest of his life, and after his death, she was instrumental in arranging his papers for various biographers and scientific colleagues.

March 14, 1929, was Einstein's fiftieth birthday. To escape the anticipated crowd of well-wishers and journalists, he left his Berlin apartment and went into hiding for the day in the home of his doctor, Janos Plesch. For the occasion, the German government decided to honor Einstein by building him a small cottage outside Berlin as a place of rest and retreat.

But the ensuing difficulties revealed something of the uncertain attitude of the Germans toward their most famous scientist. After several false starts, they selected a plot of land in the suburb of Caputh. No sooner had they done so than right-wing elements in the government began to question the gift. Seized by collective indecision, the government failed to build the house, so the Einsteins financed it out of their personal savings. In spite of the embarassing circumstances, the Einsteins loved their cottage in Caputh, surrounded as it was by beautiful lakes where Einstein could enjoy his new sailboat, the *Tummler*, another birthday gift.

The year 1929 was also the year of the stock market crash in the United States and the beginning of a worldwide economic depression. Thousands of unemployed and disaffected Germans were drawn to the Nazi party, which blamed the Jews, liberals, intellectuals, pacifists, and communists for all of Germany's problems. Einstein was often singled out by the fascists as a hated symbol of all these groups, and he had good reason to fear for his life.

The depression sealed the fate of the fragile Weimar republic. The German experiment in democratic reform was coming to an end.

During this period of time, Einstein ended his frustrating on-again, off-again relationship with the League of Nations and its Committee on Intellectual Cooperation. The League had done virtually nothing to alleviate the conditions that were driving Germany into the hands of the fascists. Einstein's advocacy of pacifism and internationalism, his calls for young men to refuse military service, were generally regarded as naive by Europe's statesmen.

But Einstein did perform one final service for the committee by participating in its program for publishing the views of leading intellectuals. He and Sigmund Freud wrote a series of letters to each other on the question of how to end war, which the committee published in 1933 under the title *Why War?* The discussion had a cheerless quality, however. Einstein blamed the ruling classes and their control of the schools and the press for encouraging national hatreds. The aging and disillusioned Freud, on the other hand, expressed no hope that aggression and irrationality could be eliminated from the human psyche. As if to prove his point, Germany banned the pamphlet.

In the early 1930s, Einstein made several short trips to the United States as a visiting professor at the California Institute of Technology in Pasadena. In the United States, he made many friends within the scientific community, and in view of what was happening in Germany, he was greatly impressed by the strength and stability of American democracy.

In Hollywood he met, among others, the writer Upton Sinclair and the actor-director Charlie Chaplin. He attended a special screening of Louis Wolheim's new anti-war film, already banned in Germany, *All Quiet on the Western Front*. He met the aging Albert Michelson, whose interferometer experiments had revealed the constancy of the speed of light almost fifty years earlier.

He also met the astronomer Edwin Hubble, whose work with the 100-inch Mount Wilson telescope high in the Sierra Madre was helping to extend Einstein's ideas into the field of *cosmology*, the study of the shape and evolution of the universe as a whole. When Einstein first proposed general relativity, astronomers knew little about the universe beyond our own galaxy and assumed that its structure was stable. Einstein's equations implied that the universe is not stable, but should be expanding or contracting. Einstein had introduced into his equations a mathematical term, the "cosmological constant," to correct for this unexpected result. But Hubble showed that the distant galaxies are indeed spreading away from each other. Einstein later called the cosmological constant the greatest mistake of his life.

Returning to Germany from one of his Pasadena trips, Einstein noted that conditions were worsening. He wrote to a friend in England, "The situation here is horrible. All money values have disappeared, and the people are disturbed and embittered against the government. The future that lies ahead is threatening and dark."[2]

Charlie Chaplin (right) escorted Einstein and Elsa to a premiere of a movie he directed.

Einstein delivers an address before the Academic Assistance Council.

In 1932, the American educator Abraham Flexner visited Einstein in Caputh and suggested that he come to America permanently as a member of a new Institute of Advanced Study that Flexner wanted to create at Princeton University in New Jersey. Einstein did not immediately accept, but kept the offer in mind. He was lecturing in Pasadena in January 1933 when Adolf Hitler was appointed chancellor of Germany. After Hitler assumed dictatorial powers in March, Einstein traveled to the German consulate in New York and announced that he would not return to Germany.

He returned instead to Belgium, where, as a result of his participation in the Solvay Congresses, he had formed a close friendship with the Belgian royal family. He settled into the small resort town of Le Coq-sur-mer. The Belgian Queen Elizabeth assigned him two bodyguards and forbade the residents of the town to give out his address.

Back in Germany, the Nazis looted his house in Caputh and seized his bank accounts. His scientific writings went up in flames at public book burnings, along with the works of Thomas Mann, Sigmund Freud, Stefan Zweig, and Erich Maria Remarque. Under pressure from the Nazi government, the Prussian Academy of Sciences considered expelling Einstein. This created a terrible dilemma for Max Planck, who had brought Einstein to Germany and had repeatedly urged him to stay. To save his friend embarassment, Einstein voluntarily resigned from the academy.

Planck's situation was tragic, but of his own making. His sense of duty to his nation and his innate respect for authority had blinded him to what was about to happen. The revered discoverer of the quantum detested the Nazis, but could not bring himself to believe that they would stay in power or that the situation in Germany would become intolerable. He made a number of patriotic statements that chilled Einstein.

But when Planck met with Hitler and tried to explain that it would be bad for German science if politics dictated what theories scientists could investigate, Hitler rudely told him that if it were not for his age he would be in a concentration camp. Planck stayed in Germany throughout the coming war, in disfavor and increasingly isolated from his scientific colleagues. His son was executed for participating in a plot by German generals to assassinate Hitler late in the war. Planck lived until 1947, and he had the grim satisfaction of watching the Third Reich crumble around him.

While Einstein was in Belgium, two young conscientious objectors were arrested by the Belgian authorities for refusing military service. Their supporters approached Einstein and asked him what they should do if war came. Einstein had been an uncompromising pacifist up to this time. He had signed petitions with the Indian political leader Mohandas K. Ghandi pledging to resist military service. But the situation in Germany and the growing persecution of the Jews forced him to reconsider his position. He astonished his listeners by saying that under the circumstances, it was time to fight. From this point on, Einstein's hostility toward the Germans knew no bounds, and even after the war he never forgave them.

In June 1933 the Einsteins, Helen Dukas, and Einstein's assistant, Walter Mayer, left Belgium for England. Here Einstein raised money to help scholars, Jews, and other refugees escape from Germany through the Academic Assistance Council, led by Ernest Rutherford and William Beveridge, director of the London School of Economics. Einstein's group then left England and arrived in the United States on October 17, 1933. Einstein had accepted Flexner's offer to come to Princeton. He would never set foot in Europe again.

NINE

COMING TO AMERICA

The arrival of Einstein in the United States was a coup for American science, and the event was duly celebrated in the press. He was not the only one making the journey, however. Many scientists were fleeing Germany or the other nations of Europe in anticipation of Nazi persecutions and war.

The nuclear physicist Enrico Fermi came from the University of Rome in Mussolini's Italy, where he had been bombarding uranium atoms with *neutrons*, a new subatomic particle discovered by the English physicist James Chadwick in 1932. Though the implications of this work were not yet fully understood, Fermi received the Nobel Prize for it in 1938. At the award ceremony, he refused to give the fascist salute. Fermi and his wife, who was Jewish, fled to the United States when Mussolini began to adopt Hitler's anti-Semitic policies.

From the University of Berlin came the Hungarian-born physicist Leo Szilard. He saw more clearly than others the direction nuclear research was taking, and in 1939 he convinced American physicists to stop publishing their work in this area. Another Hungarian-born physicist, Edward Teller,

Einstein in 1934

arrived in 1935. Leopold Infeld arrived from Poland in 1936, went to Princeton, and the next year co-authored with Einstein *The Evolution of Physics*.

The physicist Hans Bethe left Munich in 1933 and wound up at Cornell University. He eventually described the exact mechanics of nuclear fusion, the process that produces the Sun's energy by joining two hydrogen atoms to form a helium atom. German physicist Wolfgang Pauli joined Einstein at the Institute of Advanced Study in Princeton. Pauli's exclusion principle improved scientists' understanding of the energy levels in Bohr's atom.

Others did not get as far as America. Max Born, the discoverer of probability waves, fled to Scotland, as did Erwin Finlay-Freundlich. Erwin Schrödinger went to Ireland.

In January 1934, four months after Einstein's arrival, President Franklin Delano Roosevelt invited him to be an overnight guest at the White House. By the fall of 1935, the Einsteins were settled in Princeton and had moved into a modest, two-story house at 112 Mercer Street, a sleepy, tree-lined street within walking distance of the new Institute of Advanced Study. Here Einstein would spend the rest of his life, working without success to find the unified field theory and making occasional attacks on what he regarded as the incompleteness of quantum theory.

In September 1936 Einstein learned of the death of his old friend Marcel Grossman, and in December of that year his wife, Elsa, died. He was not left alone, however, for his stepdaughter Margot had joined him in Princeton the year before, and his secretary, Helen Dukas, assumed many of his wife's housekeeping duties. His sister, Maja, arrived in Princeton in 1939.

His daily routine in Princeton was fairly simple. He had few official responsibilities. In the mornings he would walk to the Institute for discussions with his colleagues. At noon, he would return to his home, usually for a lunch of pasta, which he had learned to love as a young man staying with his parents in Italy. After lunch, he might take a nap or do some

*Helen Dukas, Einstein, and his stepdaughter Margot Einstein
became U.S. citizens in 1940.*

work in his study on the second floor. A typical dinner con-
sisted of cold sandwiches, after which he might continue to
work, entertain guests, or play the violin.

Occasionally, delighted undergraduates would see him wan-
dering the Princeton campus in sandals and a shabby sweater,
eating an ice cream cone. He also enjoyed long rides in an
open convertible, chauffered by his friend, the radiologist Gustav Bucky. In the summers, he tended to vacation somewhere
near Long Island Sound where he could do some sailing.

The World War II Years

Meanwhile, in Europe, Hitler's aggression had escalated to
world war. By 1939, the normally pacifist Einstein was sign-
ing a letter urging President Roosevelt to develop an atomic

bomb. News of German research convinced him of the necessity of this action. The news came through the Jewish physicist Lise Meitner, who had fled Germany for Sweden but continued to correspond with her former coworker at the Kaiser Wilhelm Institute in Berlin, the chemist Otto Hahn.

Hahn told Meitner about an experiment in which his team bombarded uranium with neutrons, as Fermi had done. The researchers were surprised to find that two lighter elements had been produced. It dawned on Meitner that these results contained the potential for a fission bomb. If, as the uranium nuclei split, neutrons are emitted, a chain reaction could be initiated from uranium atom to uranium atom, releasing tremendous amounts of energy. In fact, Einstein's formula $E = mc^2$ could be used to calculate the energy.

Bohr relayed Meitner's concept of fission to American scientists at the Fifth Congress on Theoretical Physics in Washington, D.C. The scientists raced back to their laboratories and confirmed Hahn's experiments. That Germany might be ahead in the development of a fission weapon was deeply disturbing, especially to the refugee scientists who sensed Hitler's intentions. They knew that Germany had stopped the sale of uranium from the mines it had seized when it had taken over Czechoslovakia.

In July 1939 three men—Leo Szilard, Edward Teller, and Eugene Wigner—visited Einstein, who was then vacationing at Nassau Point on Long Island. They asked him to write a letter to President Roosevelt alerting him to the importance of the research the Germans were doing. In the letter, dated August 2, 1939, Einstein talked about "extremely powerful bombs of a new type" and urged "quick action on the part of the administration."

The degree of influence Einstein had in initiating the U.S. work on developing the atomic bomb is open to debate. Szilard gave the letter to the economist Alexander Sachs, a close friend of the President. The pressure of events prevented Roosevelt from meeting with Sachs until October, but as soon as the meeting took place, the President acted. The first step was the creation of the Briggs committee to supervise and coordinate nuclear research at various American universities. The Briggs committee was eventually merged with the Office of Scientific Research and Development. By the middle of 1942, the government was fully committed to the development of an atomic bomb through a program known as the Manhattan Project, directed by the physicist J. Robert Oppenheimer and Brigadier General Leslie B. Groves of the Army Corps of Engineers.

Einstein's involvement in the actual building of the bomb was minor. When asked, he contributed some ideas on a method of separating uranium isotopes by a process called gaseous diffusion, in which uranium is evaporated to form a gas. He was never formally told what the process would be used for, though it is difficult to believe he didn't know. The truth is that building the bomb was a job for younger scientists. When the test bomb was exploded in the Alamogordo desert, Einstein was sixty-six years old and not in the best of health. He was, at any rate, more interested in theoretical than practical work.

It is also true that within certain sections of the government, Einstein was not fully trusted. He was a socialist, and except for his hatred of the Nazis he was a pacifist who had encouraged war resisters. He was known to have advocated the free exchange of scientific information—an appalling idea to any self-respecting intelligence agency, and the Manhattan Project was the greatest of all wartime secrets. Would such a man say the wrong thing to one of his many friends and visitors? He was diplomatically kept at a distance.

Einstein did wish to make a contribution to the war effort, however, so he agreed to work as a consultant for the U.S. Navy Bureau of Ordnance. Twice a month, George Gamow, who would later popularize the "big bang" theory of the origin of the universe, traveled from Washington to Princeton to show Einstein various schemes for new types of bombs and underwater mines. Einstein reviewed the plans and approved

Sailing was one of Einstein's hobbies.

those he thought practical, just as if he were back in the patent office at Bern.

In November 1943 he was asked to donate his original handwritten 1905 paper on special relativity to an auction to raise money for war bonds. He had not saved the original paper, so Helen Dukas dictated the published version to him while he wrote out a new copy in his own hand. At the auction in February 1944, the Kansas City Insurance Company paid $6.5 million for the manuscript and then donated it to the Library of Congress.

In April 1945 Germany, besieged by British, American, and Russian armies, surrendered after Adolf Hitler committed suicide. It quickly became evident that the German atomic research program, under the direction of Werner Heisenberg, had come to nothing. In the last year of the war, Germany did not have the time and could not spare its dwindling resources and industrial capacity to gamble on the success of such a project. "This situation," Heisenberg wrote, "spared the German physicists the decision whether to plead for an attempt to produce atom bombs."[1]

If failure brought the Germans a salve for their consciences, success had the opposite effect in the United States. The question of using atom bombs in the continuing war with Japan was still very much alive. With Germany out of the war and fascism destroyed, a number of scientists who worked on the bomb began to have doubts about using it to end the war with Japan.

A memorandum was prepared and signed by the scientists who saw the atomic bomb not just as another weapon, but as an ultimate weapon of such destructive force that it could end civilization. They knew that the secrets of atomic energy could be worked out by the scientists and technicians of any moderately industrialized nation. If the use of nuclear weapons was accepted as just another way of making war, they believed controlling such weapons in the post-war world would be a serious problem.

Leo Szilard was prominent among the dissenters, and he

hoped to express his concerns directly to Roosevelt. He had another letter from Einstein. Einstein could not directly admit to having guessed what kind of weapon was being developed, but he expressed in guarded language his support for Szilard's views. The meeting with the president was scheduled for May 8, 1945, but Roosevelt died on April 12, and the new president, Harry Truman, was not sympathetic to Szilard's appeal. On August 6 an atomic bomb was detonated over the Japanese city of Hiroshima, and on August 9 a second bomb was dropped on the city of Nagasaki. More than 120,000 people were killed instantly in the two cities, and Japan surrendered.

Fighting for Peace

In April 1945 Einstein retired from his position at the Institute of Advanced Study, though he remained in Princeton and continued to use the institute's offices for his research into the unified field theory. In 1946 his sister, Maja, suffered a stroke. Einstein spent many hours reading to her as she endured increasing paralysis, and she finally died in 1951.

As he thought more and more about the atomic bomb and the post-war rivalry between the United States and the Soviet Union, Einstein felt compelled to speak out publicly about the dangers of nuclear weapons. In 1946, when dissident Manhattan Project scientists formed the Emergency Committee of Atomic Scientists to protest the spread of nuclear weapons, Einstein was elected the committee's president. Szilard, Hans Bethe, and the chemists Harold Urey and Linus Pauling were also members of the group.

The committee began publishing the *Bulletin of the Atomic Scientists*, giving the scientific community a voice on political issues. It became famous for the image of a clock printed on its cover with a changing minute hand. The minute hand was positioned close to or far away from midnight—nuclear doomsday—depending on the editors' assessment of the current state of world tensions.

A meeting of the Emergency Committee of Atomic Scientists in November 1946 included Harold Urey, seated to the left; Selig Hecht, seated to the right; and standing from left to right, Victor Weisskopf, Leo Szilard, Hans Bethe, Thorfin Hogness, and Philip Morse.

Einstein wrote a number of articles for the *Bulletin* and for other journals during this period, arguing for a single world government with the power to halt aggression. In 1947 he wrote an "Open Letter" to the General Assembly of the United Nations making the same points. He was criticized by conservatives in Congress as a communist and a "foreign-born agitator."

Others thought he was simply naive, but it was in his character to aim for fundamental principles, to ignore the political complexities that prevented others from finding solutions. He was an idealist in the sense that he believed that the same logic he applied to scientific problems could be used to solve human problems, and he refused to allow prejudice, passion, narrow self-interest, or the intrigues of politicians to deflect him from his conclusions. For millions of people during this time, he became the conscience of a war-weary world, warning that human society was not yet mature enough to control the power that science had given it.

His writings showed that his concept of pacifism had evolved. Before Hitler came to power, he believed that there was no justification for war, and that if just a small percentage of the able-bodied men in all the belligerent countries refused military service, aggression could be stopped. These views endeared Einstein to many organizations of pacifists and war resisters in the years between the world wars. But they regarded his wartime views as a betrayal.

Einstein had come to believe that force is sometimes necessary to stop aggression. "Organized power can be opposed only by organized power," he said. "Much as I regret this, there is no other way."[2] He felt that the use of force is justified if sanctioned by a broad coalition of democratic nations or a world government. The new threat of nuclear weapons made world unity and an international police force more urgent, he felt. In view of the extermination of the Jews, he believed that it might even be justifiable for a world authority to forcefully intervene in the internal affairs of a nation to stop oppression or genocide.

There was one hatred that he could not overcome. He could never forgive the Germans. After World War I, in spite of his distaste for Prussian militarism and the rising right wing, he had pleaded for German inclusion in European affairs and had used his prestige to break down animosities. He would not be fooled again. The extermination of the Jews was unforgivable, and he had come to regard the Germans as profoundly evil.

He was appalled by American and British efforts to rearm and reindustrialize Germany as a bulwark against the Soviet Union. In 1949 the Kaiser Wilhelm Institute was renamed the Max Planck Institute, and Einstein was asked to rejoin. He wrote in reply, "The crime of the Germans is truly the most abominable ever to be recorded in history. The conduct of the German intellectuals . . . was no better than that of the mob. . . . In view of these circumstances, I feel an irrepressible aversion to participating in anything that represents any aspect of public life in Germany."

In 1948 Einstein was pleased to witness the establishment of a Jewish state in Palestine, but the circumstances troubled him. Israel had been established through the displacement of many Palestinian Arabs. Einstein could never quite adopt the hard line of the Zionists toward their Arab neighbors, and though he supported the defense of the Jewish state by force, his relationship with the Zionists was often a contentious one.

Nevertheless, Einstein's prestige was so great that in late 1952, upon the death of Chaim Weitzmann, Israel's first president, Einstein was asked to replace him. Though the position of president was largely ceremonial, Einstein politely declined. He knew he was the last person in the world with the temperament or skills to become involved in politics.

The Final Years

The year 1948 brought news of the death of his first wife, Mileva, in Zurich. In the same year, Einstein underwent exploratory surgery, and doctors discovered a blockage in his abdominal artery. It was clear that his health was failing. Still, he continued to work feverishly on one set of equations after another, trying to find a connection between gravity and electromagnetism. He also struggled to find a more satisfactory explanation of quantum theory.

He continued to speak out in favor of world government and nuclear disarmament. But these appeals were being made in an increasingly hostile political environment. The absorption of eastern Europe into the Soviet bloc, the communist triumph in China in 1949, and the Korean war in 1950 made talk of international cooperation sound dangerous. These events created an anti-communist sentiment in the United States that would grow to irrational proportions.

Einstein played a part in trying to calm the irrational hysteria. In the late 1940s, the House Un-American Activities Committee under Congressman Martin Dies investigated supposed communist influence in American life. It was not hard for overzealous investigators to find "evidence" of such influence in a country that until only a few years before had been an ally of the Soviet Union. Many Americans had been attracted to radical ideas during the Depression, long before the war.

Congressman Dies led a group of ambitious politicians who built their careers by exposing the "communist menace." In 1947 the Hollywood community was investigated, and a group of screenwriters known as the Hollywood Ten were driven from their jobs because of their refusal to answer the committee's questions. This was the beginning of the blacklist, a secret list circulated to employers containing the names of people with undesirable political beliefs.

Blacklists spread throughout American life as unscrupulous employers found a new tool to crush dissent and protest among their workers. Universities and unions purged themselves of suspected communists. Thousands lost their jobs, and some were sent to prison for refusing to cooperate with the witch-hunt. The situation grew worse in 1950 when the investigations of the House committee were overshadowed by those of a Senate committee chaired by Wisconsin Senator Joseph McCarthy.

Einstein watched these events with increasing disquiet. It seemed to him a chilling reminder of the Nazi attacks on intellectuals and artists during the 1920s and 1930s. He spoke out forcefully in June 1953 when a Brooklyn teacher, William Frauenglass, who had been called to defend his leftist beliefs before Congress, approached Einstein for help. Einstein wrote Frauenglass a letter of support and told him that the letter "need not be considered 'confidential.'"

The letter was published in the *New York Times*. "What ought the minority of intellectuals to do against this evil?" Einstein asked. "Frankly, I can only see the revolutionary way of noncooperation in the sense of Gandhi's. Every intellectual who is called before one of the committees ought to refuse to testify, i.e., he must be prepared for jail and economic ruin, in short for the sacrifice of his personal welfare in the interests of the cultural welfare of his country."[3]

McCarthyism continued to take its toll. In 1954, attention began to focus on J. Robert Oppenheimer, head of the Manhattan Project. After the war, Oppenheimer became an advocate of the international control of nuclear weapons and advised against the development of the hydrogen bomb. In 1947 Oppenheimer had accepted the directorship of the Institute of Advanced Study in Princeton, and he became Einstein's neighbor. Now Oppenheimer's liberal views and his past political associations brought him under the scrutiny of the Atomic Energy Commission, prodded by McCarthy's committee. Einstein defended Oppenheimer in the newspapers in April 1954, but it had little effect. The AEC judged Oppenheimer "a loyal citizen but not a good security risk," and the man who knew everything there was to know about the building of the atomic bomb was forbidden access to classified information.

In March 1953, on the occasion of his seventy-fourth birthday, Einstein received an unexpected treat. From Paris came a postcard of the Notre Dame cathedral, addressed to the "President of the Olympia Academy." Two of his oldest friends from his student days in Zurich, Conrad Habicht and Maurice Solovine, had survived all of Europe's troubles and were sending him birthday greetings. The postcard cheered Ein-

Einstein and J. Robert Oppenheimer

stein, but it must also have reminded him of the passage of the years and his own failing health. The time remaining for scientific work was precious.

At the time, Einstein was suffering from hemolytic anemia as well as heart and stomach problems, and his life settled into a quiet routine with frequent bed rest. He was not the best patient. As one friend put it, his doctor forbade him to buy tobacco—but not to steal it. Einstein had one last meeting with Bohr in 1954, in which the two men argued good-naturedly about quantum physics.

News of the death of his friend Michele Besso came in March 1955. Einstein signed his last letter on April 11, 1955. It was a reply to the British philosopher Bertrand Russell, agreeing to support a manifesto protesting the nuclear arms race.

On April 13, 1955, Einstein was stricken with severe abdominal pains and two days later was taken to a hospital in Princeton. An aneurysm in his aorta was about to rupture. At the time, operations to correct such problems were very risky, and he refused surgery, though death was certain without it. His son, Hans Albert, who had graduated from the ETH and was a professor of physics at the University of California at Berkeley, rushed to his side. His stepdaughter Margot was there, along with Helen Dukas, and two old friends, Gustav Bucky and Otto Nathan.

For several days Einstein lingered on, haggard and in pain, knowing that he was dying, but cheerful and calm. He asked Helen Dukas to bring his latest calculations to the hospital so that he might get a little more work done. He spoke at length to his last visitors about the state of science, the dimming prospects for arms control, and his growing pessimism about American democracy, which he believed was being eroded by an increasingly militaristic interpretation of national goals. On April 18, 1955, at the age of seventy-six, he died just before midnight.

After a small funeral service that included only eleven people, his body was cremated and his ashes were scattered in secret so that there would be no gravesite where worshippers could gather. His brain was removed before the cremation, but the doctors who examined it found nothing anatomically extraordinary. As Einstein had once said, "I have no special talents; I am merely intensely curious." He had also asked that the Mercer Street house not be turned into a museum. Helen Dukas and his stepdaughter Margot continued to live in the house until their deaths. Dukas died in 1982 and Margot Einstein in 1986.

Einstein's Legacy

All his adult life, all he ever really wanted was to be left alone to think. Thinking about science was so pleasurable to him that he often felt guilty about being paid to do it. There could be no higher calling than such self-absorption, no greater fascination than contemplating the "extra-personal," as he called it, and no greater reward than the reward of scientific discovery. Nothing else in life mattered as much.

And yet a lot did matter. Because his discoveries were so profound, he found it impossible to remain walled up within the world of science. The world had elevated him to the role of sage and prophet, a role he always approached with caution, humility, and humor, but a role he could not ignore. He promoted a simple faith—that war and the regimentation of human conduct were wrong, that science and culture transcended national differences, that society should distribute its goods fairly, that our control over nature was outrunning our ability to control our passions and prejudices, and that nations would have to surrender some of their sovereignty to ensure peace. For these simple ideas, he was attacked by the world's tyrants and driven from the country of his birth.

As a scientist, his methods were those of the theorist rather than the experimenter. He conjured up in his mind a bold new image of physical reality and challenged the experimenters and mathematicians to confirm what he intuitively knew to be true. In the words of his biographer Banesh Hoffman, "He was at heart an artist, employing the medium of science." Later, when the experimenters and mathematicians buried themselves in quantum numbers and shunned any conception of physical reality beyond what they chose to observe, his artist's soul rebelled.

In everyday experience, Newton's laws work well enough

Einstein at Princeton

and are still used widely by scientists and engineers. They are accurate and reliable enough to plot the trajectory of an artillery shell and even the trajectory of a spacecraft moving through the solar system. But today the theory of relativity is no longer a fascinating abstraction. It has many applications in the most advanced areas of science. When, for example, physicists design magnets to deflect the path of a subatomic particle moving close to the speed of light in a particle accelerator, they must take into account the particle's increased mass according to relativity theory. If they used Newton's laws, the magnetic force would not be large enough.

Experiments have borne out some of Einstein's strangest predictions. For instance, two very accurate atomic clocks were set to the same time, and then one clock was carried in a high-speed airplane around the world. When the two clocks were compared, the fast-moving clock recorded less elapsed time than the other clock. In fact, some satellites must correct for the reduced ticking rate of their clocks when they send data to Earth.

Another remarkable confirmation of the theory has to do with subatomic particles called *muons* that are generated in the upper atmosphere. They have a half-life of only 1.5 microseconds, which means that half of them decay into another particle in that time period. It takes about 6 microseconds for them to reach Earth, so only one-sixteenth of the original number of muons should survive at the surface. But because they travel close to the speed of light, we perceive their time of existence as being stretched out about four times as long. So taking relativity into consideration, we should find that one-half of the muons reach Earth. Scientists have confirmed that one-half, rather than one-sixteenth, of the original number of muons reach Earth.

Modern cosmology draws heavily on the theory of relativity to explain such strange new phenomena as neutron stars, massive galaxies acting as "gravitational lenses," and black holes. These are all now explained in terms of space-time folding in on itself. Physicists and astronomers use general relativity to discuss the shape of the entire universe, whether it is "positively" or "negatively" curved, whether it will expand forever or begin to contract, how much and what kind of matter must exist to bring about expansion or contraction, and how many dimensions of space-time we all move through.

We are now aware that the fundamental qualities from which we construct our everyday experiences—space, time, matter, and energy—are really elastic qualities that vary depending on our point of view in the universe. And when we look out into this universe, we see a place where space and time can twist and bend, producing strange phenomena undreamed of before Einstein. In the same way that Copernicus and Galileo showed that Earth is not at the physical center of the universe, Einstein showed that human perceptions of the universe are themselves affected by our point of view, and that the cosmos is far richer in mysteries than anyone had imagined.

GLOSSARY

absolute space   a stationary reference volume of space specified by Isaac Newton as a reference point from which to measure the motion of planets, solar systems, and galaxies.

absolute time   a reference time specified by Isaac Newton as measured in unvarying increments from the beginning of creation.

Brownian motion   the random movement of particles suspended in a liquid or a gas resulting from the collisions of molecules.

cosmology   a branch of astronomy dealing with the origin and history of the universe.

dynamo   a machine that produces electricity by rotating coils of wire in a magnetic field. It is also known as an electrical generator.

electromagnetic field   the portion of space surrounding magnets and charged wires that contains electric and magnetic energy. Electromagnetic energy also travels through space in the form of radio waves, visible light, X rays, microwaves, and more.

ether   an invisible substance that in the nineteenth century was believed to permeate the universe and transmit light.

gymnasium   a European secondary school that prepares students for the university.

inertia   the tendency of matter to remain motionless or to move at a steady speed, unless acted on by an outside force.

inertial frame of reference   a system at rest or moving at a constant speed in a straight line.

interferometer   an instrument developed by Albert Michelson and Edward Morley to detect the ether. It measures extremely small distances based on an interference pattern of light waves.

kinetics   a branch of science that deals with the physical effects of the motions of atoms and molecules on a body or system.

magnetic field   the portion of space surrounding magnets and current-carrying wires that contains magnetic force.

mass   a quantity of matter. It is a measure of matter's inertia. A mass has weight as a result of gravity.

matter-waves   entities that have characteristics of both waves and particles.

mechanics   a branch of physics that deals with forces and energy and their effect on bodies.

medium   a substance that transmits waves or vibrations.

perihelion   the point in a planet's orbit that is closest to the Sun.

photon   a particle of light equivalent to a quantum of electromagnetic energy.

principle of complementarity   the idea proposed by Neils Bohr that the particle and wave characteristics of light are complementary, rather than contradictory, and that they are a function of the measurement technique.

principle of equivalence   Einstein's finding that an object in gravity is indistinguishable from an object accelerating at the rate of gravity. It is the cornerstone of the general theory of relativity.

privatdozent   a German word for a university teacher who is paid by each student, rather than the university.

quanta   the smallest increments of energy that light can be divided into.

quantum mechanics   a theory of matter that describes the behavior of subatomic particles based on the idea that they have properties of both waves and particles.

redshift   the shift of light toward longer wavelengths that results from relative motion (the Doppler effect) or from the gravitational field of the source.

relativity of simultaneity   the principle that says that the measurement of time is relative because of the relative motion of people and systems. As a result, no two events can be guaranteed to occur simultaneously.

self-inductance   a property of an electric circuit by which it induces a voltage in itself as a result of carrying a changing current.

simultaneity   see *relativity of simultaneity*.

statistical mechanics   a branch of mechanics that applies statistics to determine the motion of a system having a large number of parts.

stimulated emission   the emission of photons by atoms after they have been stimulated by photons, as opposed to the spontaneous emission that occurs naturally. Stimulated emission is the basis of the operation of the laser.

tensor calculus   a type of mathematics that uses tensors, vectors that can describe objects in four dimensions.

time dilation   the slowing of time that an observer perceives in a system that is moving with respect to him or her. It is usually noticeable only when the system is moving at speeds approaching the speed of light.

uncertainty principle   a quantum mechancal principle proposed by Werner Heisenberg. It says it is impossible to determine simultaneously the position and momentum of a subatomic particle such as an electron with high accuracy.

unified field theory   a theory that physicists are working on that would unify the equations for the four known types of forces in the universe: electromagnetism, gravity, and the strong force and the weak force, which bind particles together in atomic nuclei.

Source Notes

Ronald W. Clark's *Einstein: The Life and Times* is an excellent biography of Einstein the man, but for a more comprehensive discussion of the concepts of relativity and its scientific background, Philip Frank's *Einstein: His Life and Times* and Banesh Hoffman's *Albert Einstein: Creator and Rebel* are more rewarding. Einstein's own "Autobiographical Notes," published in 1949 when he was seventy years old, is less a real biography than a review of the growth of his scientific thinking and the influences upon it, though it does provide some interesting anecdotes about his early years. This essay is found in Paul Schilpp's *Albert Einstein: Philosopher-Scientist*, which also contains a bibliography of Einstein's major scientific papers listed by year of publication.

Abraham Pais's *'Subtle Is the Lord . . .'* contains many useful details about Einstein's life, but one must search for them within some highly technical discussions. A lot of interesting material about Einstein's later years at Princeton can be found in Peter Bucky's *The Private Albert Einstein*. Much of Einstein's writings about politics, ethics, and society can be found in the anthologies *Ideas and Opinions, Out of My Later Years,* and *The World As I See It.*

Many of Einstein's original papers remain in special archives in Princeton, Jerusalem, and Zurich. A massive effort by scholars at Boston University to publish Einstein's Collected Papers has been underway since 1987, when the first volume was published. Information about many of the other scientists mentioned in this book can be found in Asimov's *Biographical Encyclopedia of Science and Technology*. A good general account of the history of the German Empire, the First World War, the Weimar Republic, and the rise of fascism can be found in *A History of the Modern World*, by R. R. Palmer and Joel Colton.

Two excellent popular explanations of relativity are in Stan Gibilisco's *Understanding Einstein's Theories of Relativity* and Lewis Caroll Epstein's *Relativity Visualized*. *Einstein for Beginners*, by Joseph Schwartz and Michael McGuiness, is a delightful and useful book, but covers only the theory of special relativity. Readers are encouraged to try Robert Lawson's translation of Einstein's *Relativity: The Special and the General Theory*, a popular explanation written in 1916 that conveys the simplicity, logic, and exactness of Einstein's own prose style. Two excellent books on quantum theory are Fred Wolf's *Taking the Quantum Leap* and the late Heinz Pagel's *The Cosmic Code*.

All these books are listed with publication information in For Further Reading.

Chapter 1

1. Maja Einstein letter, as quoted in Highfield and Carter, *The Private Lives of Albert Einstein*. (New York: St. Martin's Press, 1993), p. 12.
2. Albert Einstein's "Autobiographical Notes," as published in Schilpp, Paul Arthur, ed. *Albert Einstein: Philosopher-Scientist*. (La Salle, Illinois: Open Court, 1970), p. 9.
3. Clark, Ronald W. *Einstein: The Life and Times*. (New York: Avon Books, 1971), pp. 29-30.
4. Frank, Philipp. *Einstein: His Life and Times*. (New York: Da Capo Press Inc., 1947), p. 11.
5. Hoffman, Banesh. *Albert Einstein: Creator and Rebel*. (New York: Plume Books, 1972), p. 26.
6. "Autobiographical Notes," Schilpp, p. 5.
7. Albert Einstein letter, as quoted in Hoffman, p. 25.

Chapter 2

1. "Autobiograhical Notes," Schilpp, p. 21.
2. Clark, p. 61.
3. "Autobiographical Notes," Schilpp, p. 17.

Chapter 5

1. Pais, Abraham. *'Subtle Is the Lord . . .': The Science and the Life of Albert Einstein.* (New York: Oxford University Press, 1982) p. 152.
2. Clark, p. 174.

Chapter 6

1. Hoffman, p. 132.
2. Ibid, p. 133.

Chapter 7

1. Frank, Phillip. *Einstein: His Life and Times*, p. 160.
2. Clark, p. 468, 469.
3. Pais, p. 114.

Chapter 8

1. Pais, p. 416.
2. Clark, p. 534.

Chapter 9

1. Clark, p. 703.
2. O. Nathan and M. Norden, *Einstein on Peace.* (New York: Schocken, 1968), p. 236.
3. Hoffman, pp. 246–7.

FOR FURTHER READING

Asimov, Isaac. *Asimov's Biographical Encyclopedia of Science and Technology*, 2d ed. Garden City: Doubleday, 1982.

———— *Understanding Physics*. Vol. 1, *Motion, Sound, and Heat*. New York: Mentor Books, 1966.

———— *Understanding Physics*. Vol. 2, *Light, Electricity, and Magnetism*. New York: Mentor Books, 1966.

———— *Understanding Physics*. Vol. 3, *The Electron, Proton, and Neutron*. New York: Mentor Books, 1966.

Barnett, Lincoln. *The Universe and Dr. Einstein*. New York: Mentor Books, 1962.

Bucky, Peter A. *The Private Albert Einstein*. Kansas City: Andrews and McMeel, 1992.

Calder, Nigel. *Einstein's Universe*. New York: Viking Press, 1979.

Clark, Ronald W. *Einstein: The Life and Times*. New York: Avon Books, 1971.

Davies, Paul. *Superforce: The Search for a Grand Unified Theory of Nature*. New York: Simon & Schuster, 1984.

Einstein, Albert. *Ideas and Opinions*. New York: Crown Publishers, 1954.

———— *Out of My Later Years*. New York: Citadel Press, 1991.

———— *Relativity: The Special and the General Theory*. New York: Crown Publishers, 1961.

———— *The World As I See It*. New York: Citadel Press, 1991.

Einstein, Albert, and Leopold Infeld. *The Evolution of Physics*. New York: Simon & Schuster, 1966.

Epstein, Lewis Carroll. *Relativity Visualized*. San Francisco: Insight Press, 1992.

Frank, Philipp. *Einstein: His Life and Times*. New York: Da Capo Press, Inc., 1947.

Gamow, George. *Mr. Tompkins in Paperback*. Cambridge: Cambridge University Press, 1993.

Gibilisco, Stan. *Understanding Einstein's Theories of Relativity: Man's Perspective on the Cosmos*. New York: Dover Books, 1991.

Gribbin, John. *In Search of Schrodinger's Cat: Quantum Physics and Reality*. New York: Bantam Books, 1984.

Highfield, Roger, and Paul Carter. *The Private Lives of Albert Einstein*. New York: St. Martin's Press, 1993.

Hoffman, Banesh. *Albert Einstein: Creator and Rebel*. New York: Plume Books, 1972.

Pagels, Heinz R. *The Cosmic Code: Quantum Physics as the Language of Nature*. New York: Simon & Schuster, 1982.

Pais, Abraham. *'Subtle is the Lord . . .': The Science and the Life of Albert Einstein*. New York: Oxford University Press, 1982.

Palmer, R. R., and Joel Colton. *A History of the Modern World*, 2d ed. New York: McGraw-Hill, 1992.

Sayen, Jamie. *Einstein in America*. New York: Crown Publishers, 1985.

Schilpp, Paul Arthur, ed. *Albert Einstein: Philosopher-Scientist*. La Salle, Illinois: Open Court, 1970. (This volume contains Einstein's "Autobiographical Notes.")

Schwartz, Joseph, and Michael McGuiness. *Einstein for Beginners*. New York: Pantheon Books, 1979.

Tauber, Gerald, ed. *Albert Einstein's Theory of General Relativity: 60 Years of Its Influence on Man and the Universe*. New York: Crown Publishers, 1979.

White, Michael, and John Gribbin. *Einstein: A Life in Science*. New York: Dutton, 1993.

Wolf, Fred Allan. *Taking the Quantum Leap*. New York: Harper & Row, 1981.

Index